"Once you read Greg's latest book, *Body Language Secrets To Win More Negotiations*, and apply the easy to use strategies, you'll be able to get more out of every negotiation you are in. In addition to the easy to apply negotiation strategies, he also gives you a 'how to' to detect Body Language and other nonverbal signals whether you are negotiating in person or over the phone. With this combination, once you apply what you discover in this book, you will have a huge advantage in every aspect of your life."

—Patryk Wezowski, founder of Center for Body Language,
World's #1 Body Language Training for Business

"*Body Language Secrets To Win More Negotiations* is the ultimate guide to making better decisions, fewer mistakes, and knowing what to do when others don't have a clue. Recognizing the meaning of everyone's moves... from a flinch to a hand gesture to a half smile... is your answer to making your own super-smart moves in a negotiation."

—Greg Hague, creator of the "22-Step Home Sale Formula" featured in Forbes & 220 publications worldwide

"Greg Williams shows us every prospect is an open book in, *Body Language Secrets To Win More Negotiations*, and he just gave us the secret code. Finally, a book that shows us how they are thinking! Now you can make all the right moves and win! We always thought every shift in the chair meant something, and Greg Williams shows us what it means and how to use it! Please don't give this book "*Body Language Secrets To Win More Negotiations*," to my competitors. I want them to make all the wrong moves!"

—Jeffrey Hayzlett, primetime TV and podcast host,
Chairman C-Suite Network

Body Language Secrets

TO WIN MORE NEGOTIATIONS

* * *

HOW TO READ ANY OPPONENT AND GET WHAT YOU WANT

* * *

GREG WILLIAMS
WITH PAT IYER

B CAREER PRESS

BODY LANGUAGE SECRETS TO WIN MORE NEGOTIATIONS
EDITED BY PATRICIA KOT
TYPESET BY KRISTIN GOBLE
Cover design by Howard Grossman/12E Design
Printed in the U.S.A.

To order this title, please call toll-free 1-800-CAREER-1 (NJ and Canada: 201-848-0310) to order using VISA or MasterCard, or for further information on books from Career Press.

The Career Press, Inc.
12 Parish Drive
Wayne, NJ 07470
www.careerpress.com

Library of Congress Cataloging-in-Publication Data
CIP Data Available Upon Request.

DEDICATION

To my mother, Rosa M. Johnson, who left us in this life much too early. Thank you for the lessons you instilled in me that led to me becoming a Master Negotiator. I know you'd be proud of your baby boy for the contributions I'm making to the world.

To Milburn Preston, a man from whom I learned so much about life and manhood. Thank you. It took some time for me to grow, but I made it!

To Joel Adams, a man who enlightened me to the easy and hard lessons of reality in business and politics. I gained more insight from those lessons than you'll ever know.

I'd also like to thank my developmental editor, Pat Iyer, for her friendship and dedication to this project. Her writing abilities added immeasurable value to this book.

TABLE OF CONTENTS

INTRODUCTION

You look around the poker table. You're holding a strong hand—a pair of jacks and two sevens. The other three players have matched your last raise. Should you raise again?

To your left, Jose, the youngest player, who is wearing sunglasses to hide his eyes, taps his left thumb on the table. Across from you, Georgia absentmindedly stirs her gin and tonic. Then there's Jamal, the old fellow sitting to your right, noisily sucking on a lozenge and scratching his nose.

You go all in, pushing your whole pile of chips to the middle of the table. When Jose and Jamal fold and Georgia confidently turns over her two aces, you smile as you rake in the pot.

You won because you skillfully read your opponents' "tells," those subtle and not-so-subtle signals that inadvertently reveal peoples' thoughts and emotions. Master negotiators do the same, "reading between the lines" to detect the body language signals that will help them read the minds of their opponents. And, of course, they carefully control their own "tells" or body language.

Body Language Secrets to Win More Negotiations reveals surprising insights into the ways body language, microexpressions, and emotional intelligence influence the outcome of every negotiation. In these pages you not only will learn how to interpret nonverbal messages, but you will discover many practical tools for turning those silent cues to your advantage at the bargaining table.

What can you expect to gain from this book? *Body Language Secrets to Win More Negotiations* will help you discover what the other negotiators are revealing through body language and micro expressions. It will teach you how to control your own expressions and body language. The way you react—or don't— can make a profound difference in a deal. This book will also assist you at the negotiation table by helping you be more adept at leveraging your knowledge of emotional intelligence, negotiation ploys, and emotional hot buttons, while enhancing your ability to do so by reading body language.

Think of this book as your guide to achieve much better results in any negotiation. Through absorbing the examples, stories, exercises, and negotiation tips, you will gain many practical tools that will give you greater confidence at the negotiation table. You will discover how to skillfully read your opponent's body language and micro expressions. You will be able to answer these questions:

- How should you set the scene to incorporate subtle methods of influencing the other negotiator?
- How does color influence a negotiation?
- How can you harness emotion to direct a negotiation?
- Should you negotiate standing up or sitting down?
- What does it mean when a person looks up and to the left?
- What is a negotiator revealing when he starts to sweat?
- What could a brief frown mean?

- How can you use the affinity principle to connect with the other negotiator?
- How can you recognize an empathetic person?
- How can you tell when the other negotiator is lying?

In addition, you will

- be able to employ hidden weapons to guide successful negotiations, such as setting the scene for the negotiation;
- skillfully recognize when you or the other negotiator is using emotion to influence the outcome of the negotiation—and learn to use this knowledge to gain an advantage;
- be able to employ an arsenal of negotiation strategies—some you have never considered using before;
- adeptly shift your strategies as you read the other negotiator's signals;
- overcome common obstacles that hamper your negotiations;
- use a systematic model to plan and execute more successful negotiations; and
- triumph as you win more negotiations.

If you are seeking ways to enhance your negotiation efforts while adeptly increasing your ability to enhance aspects of your life, *Body Language Secrets to Win More Negotiations* is a must-have book for you.

Chapter 1

❋ ❋ ❋ ❋ ❋ ❋ ❋ ❋ ❋ ❋ ❋ ❋ ❋

Silent Signals:
Observing Subtle and Not-So-Subtle Cues

Director of Purchasing Sharma Modi quietly observed the vendor sitting in front of him. Bill Walters was asking Sharma to make a significant investment in his products. Sharma observed Bill's body language. Bill shifted in his seat every few minutes. His hands trembled when he reached for his coffee cup. There was a thin sheen of perspiration on his face. Sharma said, "Bill, I have a feeling this sale means a lot to you." "Oh no," Bill replied. "We have plenty of business." After thinking about what he observed, Sharma made an offer that was substantially less than what Bill requested. Bill hesitated and then said, "Fine, let's do the deal."

In this situation, Sharma noted Bill's signs of anxiety. Even though Bill actually stated that, "Oh no, we have plenty of business," that was likely not the case based on his body language. Bill truly did need the business. Sharma revised the offer based on that knowledge. In this chapter, you'll discover how to use what you sense and see in a negotiation based on the body language that you discern.

Body Language as Nonverbal Communication

Body language can be verbal and nonverbal. Nonverbal verbal communication is expressed through your voice, such as clearing your throat. You could be saying, "I'm getting choked up possibly." Your body tries to adapt to your environment, and it makes corrections and sends signals based on how you feel. That's one reason why you should always be aware of body language signals.

There are countless forms of nonverbal communication:

- head movement
- rubbing eye, fingers, hands, arm, or leg
- shifting of body, shuffling or tapping feet
- swinging leg when sitting, drumming fingers
- gesturing with hand toward or moving away
- smiling
- frowning
- scowling

Studies indicate that up to 90 percent of communication is actually transmitted via body language. Words comprise only 10% of communication. Other people observe the subtleties that your body language conveys, and thus 90% is a huge percentage of the communication process. Everyone should be astute about body language signals. You may be saying something that happens to be exactly opposite to what you really believe. Your body language will betray you. If your body language is sending a different signal, your message will be diluted simply because the body language is out of sync with what you are saying.

You are more aware of body language than you might realize. A lot of times we will talk about how we felt a certain sensation as a result of interacting with someone. We are sensing but are not truly conscious of the body language signals being projected. Also, you will hear nonverbal clues when you speak to someone over the phone. Even if you're reading, you can pick up inflections based on words and tone of the writing.

Body Language from Head to Toe

Pay attention to what people do with their hands, arms, feet, mouth, and head to become better at sensing body language. Their gestures will give you insight. I'd like you to imagine that you're standing in front of Bill, with whom you are negotiating. I am going to take you on a guided tour of what you should observe about him.

Expressing body language with the head

Someone's head gestures will definitely give you insight into what he is thinking. Tilting his head could mean that he is deliberating. It could also convey that Bill is inquisitive or in the process of trying to back away from something that has been said.

Eye movements signal thought processes. Most people will tend to look up and to the left when they are trying to recall something that has occurred in the past. You can test this by observing the person's reaction to a neutral comment. You might say something like, "We had good weather yesterday. Do you remember what the weather was like last week at this time?" Observe which direction the person looks. If he looks up and to the left, he's trying to recall. If he looks up and to the right, he could be doing the exact same thing. By establishing his baseline (i.e., which direction he looks to retrieve information), you're able to discern what the act means to him.

This reaction means you need to go further by asking another question. Ask another neutral question, such as about another experience you shared. "Do you remember when (a specific thing) happened?" Observe how Bill moves his eyes to recall the information based on your question.

When Bill looks up and to the left, you know that he is trying to recall what he actually experienced. You get the insight that more than likely this person looks up and to the left to recall information. If he is trying to remember a sound, he will tend to look directly to the left. If he is trying to think about something that's an auditory signal and he is contemplating what that was, he will tend to look down and to the left. Establish his baseline by asking different questions at different times.

Suppose you are talking to Bill about something that relates to emotion. Note what he does with his eyes. A person who is trying to get in touch with his emotions will look down and to the right. That's so important to observe when you're at the negotiation table because that will give you the insight as to how someone truly feels about an offer, a counter offer, and so on.

A person who looks directly to the right may be trying to think of a sound he has not heard before. As an example, if I said, "Imagine if a cow and a chicken were combined. What sound would it make?" Bill might tend to look to the right because he is trying to construct the sound.

Suppose he looks up and to the right. He is visually trying to create an image or a thought in his mind. You say something along the lines of, "What do you think the weather might be like next week based on what it's been like the last few days?" Watch Bill look up and to the right to try to answer that question.

I used the weather as an example, but you can observe the same thing from a negotiation perspective. Now that you have established the baseline by which Bill uses his eyes, you can then decipher to what degree he is being truthful. Ask, "Is this the best offer that you can make?" Note the direction in which he moves his eyes. Let's say he looks up and to the right. He is actually trying to construct whether or not it is the best offer.

Take it a step further. Begin your sentence with, "I understand in the past. . . ." Notice you're already given a subtle sense of direction. "I understand in the past that only 75% of your products passed the initial quality control check." Based on what you have already observed about his eye movements, you know that Bill should be looking up and to the left to recall what has occurred in the past. Instead, you watch him look up and to the right. Now you know that likely he is in the process of creating a response that may not be as accurate as he wants you to believe. You've gained insight just from watching his eye movements. Refer to Figure 1.

Be aware of head movement in combination with what Bill says. As he says, "No, that's not true," he is nodding his head forward. This is a negotiation principle that I will return to again: When there is a conflict between what someone says and what his body language reveals, always believe the body language. The body does not lie. It attempts to act per what it believes to be the truth.

While you are talking to Bill you notice that one end of his mouth is curled upward. That is a sign of contempt. He may be saying with that movement, "How dare you try to put me on the spot. Don't try to catch me like that." If he is astute at reading body language, he may also be saying, "I know exactly what you are trying to do and it's not going to work here."

Bill smiles as he's delivering his rebuttal or reply to your question. At the same time, with the smile on his face, he leans back and put his hands behind his head. He is indicating with

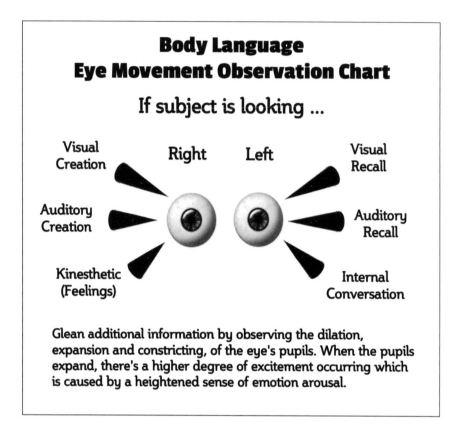

Body Language
Eye Movement Observation Chart
If subject is looking ...

Right   **Left**

Visual Creation

Auditory Creation

Kinesthetic (Feelings)

Visual Recall

Auditory Recall

Internal Conversation

Glean additional information by observing the dilation, expansion and constricting, of the eye's pupils. When the pupils expand, there's a higher degree of excitement occurring which is caused by a heightened sense of emotion arousal.

that body positioning and smile, "Okay, that's a good question. Nice try, buddy." He's literally moving away from the question, indicating that maybe you do know something or have hit a sensitive negotiating point that he would rather avoid.

Bill's hands on the back of his head are intended to tell you that he is in control of this situation. Leaning away from the question could mean he is stalling for time before he responds. Be attentive to the tone of what he says next. Suppose he says, "I'm not exactly sure that's a valid statement." Here, he is questioning the validity. Contrast that position with a different response: Bill says, "That's definitely not true." That is an emphatic statement.

Watch for clusters of gestures

Look for clusters of body language signals to confirm Bill's negotiating stance. Let's say instead of having a smile on his face he had a frown. He displayed with a frown the disdain that he had for you even posing such a question. "You don't know what you're talking about" could also be the implied meaning. Observe if he moves away from you, if he moves toward you, if he has a smile on his face, if he's frowning, if one corner of his lip is actually turned up displaying contempt, or if by chance he leans forward as he's talking.

Imagine Bill sitting at his desk. He has his hands folded on his desk as he leans forward, smiles, and says, "That's definitely not true. The most recent study showed that 95% of our products passed the initial quality control check." His hands tell you he has patience. Leaning forward tells you he confidently thinks he is in control as he confronts you or your negotiating strategy face-to-face.

The reason I'm highlighting what Bill feels is because we sometimes say, "He lied" in a situation when the data that he cited were inaccurate. In reality, that does not have to be the case even though his body language was aligned with everything that he said. Instead, he truly may not have known the answer but thought that he was telling the truth. Based on your own knowledge of the data, you might respond by saying, "Your quality control manager issued a report this year that showed the actual results were 75%." Watch Bill's body language as he responds to your statement.

There are a host of nonverbal and verbal signals. Knowing what to watch for will give you great insight into the thought process of the opposing negotiator. With such information, you'll understand to what degree his offers and counteroffers are positional. Do they set the stage for future offers/counteroffers or are they immediate reactions, such as "I better accept this offer, or I could run the risk of losing the deal"? Thus, you'll enhance your negotiation efforts and be more successful as a result of your astuteness in deciphering verbal and nonverbal signals.

How the arms convey meaning

You've learned about eye movements, head gestures, smiles, and frowns. When Bill has his arms apart, he is displaying the fact that he is really open to what it is that you and he are discussing.

Sometimes you'll see people with crossed arms. Don't be misled by this. People who are not astute at discerning body language will say, "Oh, that person's crossed arms mean that he is not receptive; he is not open." That could be the case, but remember what I said about always first establishing a foundation for how someone uses his body in situations before you start making assumptions about what one gesture means. You truly cannot reach conclusions about his demeanor from one gesture. You need to seek out the meaning from clusters of body language gestures.

As you progress in your negotiations, you observe that Bill has his arms crossed sitting opposite from you and has one leg over the other. That is more of a confirmation that he is a little closed minded and is not thinking as openly as you would like. It's an example of a cluster of gestures with both arms and legs crossed.

Because of their anatomy, women tend to cross their arms more than men. Crossing the arms could have several meanings:

- Fatigue
- Feeling cold
- Trying to get more comfortable

- Satisfaction with a point just won
- Agreement with you

Note the timing of when the person crosses his arms. If Bill crossed his arms again when a point is favorable to him, you then know Bill uses that gesture to indicate satisfaction as opposed to dissatisfaction. Observe how the person uses that gesture to determine its meaning.

Hands convey meaning

As people speak, observe if they have their palms up, indicating that they are receptive to you. Now, here's where words and body language may conflict. Suppose Bill says to you with his palms *down*, "I think this offer is going to be really good for you, and I think you should accept it." That's an incongruent message: While Bill says it is good for you, he is pushing his palms toward the floor, which conveys, "No, I don't really think it's good for you. It may be more advantageous for me." That's yet another gesture to be observant of as far as how someone uses his hands.

A good negotiator may say to you as you make your offer to him, "I think that may be a good offer for me." His hands are palms down. Consider that he may intentionally be telling you that he is not really sure if it is a good offer. He is leading you to believe that right now, but he is planning to come back and test that offer somewhere down the line.

There are so many nuances that occur when a person uses gestures. Make a conscious effort to watch your opponent's gestures to look for patterns of their use. Gestures may be related to a particular timeframe of the negotiation and be associated with clusters of other nonverbal body language. They can lead you to make some assumptions that you can test during the negotiation.

Pulling one hand back as you're speaking gives emphasis to the hand with which you are gesturing. Bill has his right palm up and his arm is back. His left hand is out and his palm is down. He says, "This is going to be the best deal that you can get. I would suggest that you take it." Bill's body language is conveying that by holding that right hand back with the palm up there may be more you can gain. His left hand extended with the palm down is indicating to you, "Actually, I want you to think this is the best deal," but the mixed message leads you to the insight that there may be more for you to gain.

Be aware that different gestures made by arms and hands convey a great deal of meaning. Properly interpreted, they reveal thought processes that can affect the negotiation.

Handshakes

Let's say Bill places one hand on top of yours. You may perceive the message from Bill as, "I'm superior to you. I'm hands up on you." You may feel patronized. That does not necessarily have to be a bad thing for you. In response, you might think to yourself, "You can feel superior to me but watch out. That will change." You may decide to display a completely different body language signal to take charge of the negotiation, which might throw Bill off course. When you note how the other negotiator shakes hands, you will get insight into what that negotiator might be thinking. Even from the handshake and the moment the negotiation process officially starts, you will get clues about Bill.

Note the firmness of a handshake. A hard handshake can convey, "Don't mess with me." A hard handshake can also be an overcompensation from a person who is weaker but does not want you to observe that he is weaker. Bill may be thinking, "I need this deal so badly. I have got to come away with this deal, but I can't show weakness." He overcompensates for that thought with a very hard handshake.

Here's what you can do when you receive a hard handshake. Offer to shake hands several times and see what happens with that handshake. If it moderates in any way, think about what is really occurring as to why the handshake has altered.

An initial handshake can be hard, soft, or limp. Does it change during the negotiation? By observing the degree it's altered, you'll gain insight into the opposing negotiator's mind-set. If you note other body language gestures (cluster of gestures) leading up to that point, you should be able to confirm his change in perspective and why it occurred. The combination of gestures will give you a sense of the direction of the other negotiator.

Using the Hand to Touch the Other Negotiator

There are certain safe parts of the body that are typically touched during a negotiation: the shoulder or elbow.

Hand on the shoulder

A person putting her hand on someone's shoulder could be indicating that she is feeling superior. You should always maintain a healthy perspective about your negotiation abilities and that of the other negotiator. Don't allow the perception of size to serve as a detriment in your negotiation efforts. For example, if you are shorter than the opposing negotiator, you can compensate for it by standing closer. You will send a subliminal message that you are not afraid to be in the other negotiator's space. If you wish not to send such a message, you can stand slightly farther away, which wouldn't amplify the height difference if you stood closer.

Touching the shoulder also may be done to comfort the other person: "Don't worry, I'll take care of this and make sure you get the best deal possible." Also, it can be a gesture of comfort, so you have to understand when it occurs as to why it's occurring. It can be a sincere gesture.

Hand on the elbow

Take note when Bill shakes your hand if he places a hand on your elbow. What that implies is extra control. While he has his hand on your elbow and shakes your hand, he can literally move your body. He could apply pressure on the elbow with his fingers and thumb to actually make you feel a sense of slight excitement or discomfort.

Imagine Bill is shaking your hand, and saying, "Don't worry about this. I'm going to make sure everything is controlled to the degree that you feel safe." While he says this, he applies a slight bit of pressure on your elbow; you may not even notice it. You will have the thought, "Yes, I don't have anything to be worried about" because he's shaking your hand while saying so, and he's literally controlling you with the soft touch that he's applying to your elbow.

Here's a countering strategy when you notice your elbow being touched in connection with a handshake. Show that you are as much in control as your opponent by putting your hand on his elbow. Observe what he does at that time. This cluster of gestures will display the mind-set more accurately as to what the other negotiator thinks in that particular situation than one gesture by itself.

Legs and Posture

Think about the last time you saw a person jiggling his leg. This is a sign of discomfort or anxiety. A person who sways as he stands may also be expressing discomfort. The swaying motion is an attempt to comfort himself. The significance of a comfort gesture depends on when it occurs in the negotiation, what has preceded it, and what gestures follow. The other negotiator may be making the gesture when the mood is light and everyone is in agreement with what's been discussed. She displays a comfort gestures which more than likely in that situation indicates she's comfortable. Contrast that with her in a confrontational environment; she feels threatened. She begins to rub her arm. In that case she's displaying a gesture to reduce the anxiety she's experiencing.

Imagine that Bill is seated across from you with one leg crossed over the other. A crossed leg could be a comfort gesture, meaning he is very comfortable with what it is that he is discussing with you or it could be a sign of discomfort. One way to discern the intent of Bill's body language is to note the degree your gestures match. If Bill has his right leg crossed and you have your right leg crossed, you are more aligned than would otherwise be the case. The two of you are really saying through your body language that you are in sync with one another. If by chance you uncross your right leg and he uncrosses his right leg, you're literally leading Bill. It means he is really in alignment with you to the point that he feels comfortable with the offer you've made, the proposal you've described, and the direction in which the negotiation is going.

Let's consider a situation in which Bill has his right leg crossed and your left leg is crossed. Your body language reveals that you are out of sync with one another.

Ankles and feet

Let's move down to the ankles and the feet. While Bill is seated, he is moving his leg around and around or forward and backward. He could indicate with that gesture that he is starting to get a little tired with the negotiation process. It can indicate, "Okay let's move it on."

To see exactly to what degree Bill may be getting tired or why a particular gesture is being used at that time, say something like, "I know a little something about body language. I thought moving your ankle and foot is a sign of anxiety." This is a negotiation ploy to get the other person to notice what he is doing and to think about *why* he is doing it. You can ask him to tell you what it means, then observe what happens next: Does he continue to move his foot around? At what point does he continue to move his foot around?

Now imagine you are talking to Bill while standing and facing him. Look at the position of his feet. Bill is more engaged in this discussion when your feet are aligned with each other. He is showing you he feels like he is on even ground. From a negotiation perspective things are progressing quite well.

Always observe someone's feet movement, be it one foot or the other even though you're looking him directly in the eye. You can still take note of what he is doing with his feet as you are engaged in the conversation. Let's say as you are discussing an aspect of the negotiation you happen to notice that Bill's foot turns away from you or points slightly in a different direction than it was when your feet were evenly aligned with each other. That positioning could indicate that Bill is growing weary. You should assess if it is from physical or mental fatigue. While you take note of when it happened, you don't have to necessarily draw attention to it. What that can also imply is Bill is letting you know he does not like your offer. Your feet, just like his perception of the deal, are now out of alignment.

You can do several things at that point. Reposition yourself as you're speaking to realign your feet with the other negotiator and then watch what he does with his left or right foot. If as you're talking he keeps it in alignment with your foot, he's signaling through his body language that he's reacting positively to what you're saying.

Suppose Bill moves his feet so that his left foot is aligned with your right foot, but his right foot is pointing in between your feet. Bill is saying he has come into agreement with you. Watch what he does with his feet as you make more proposals, because then you pinpoint his mind-set. The feet are very important in a negotiation; they give you a lot of insight into the thought process of your opponent.

Feet positioning can be part of a cluster of gestures that reveal stalling tactics. With his feet still aligned. Bill puts his right fingers up to his forehead, left hand on his hip, and starts rubbing his forehead. Although his feet are still aligned, his body language reveals this message: "I think I'm ready to conclude this deal. But I'm thinking about something else that you said and possibly trying to see how that's going to be more beneficial to you or me. Am I willing to allow that to be the case?" After Bill goes through that series of calculations, if his foot turns away from you, you are seeing his manifestation of indecisiveness with the proposal. Be astutely aware of all of those gestures and clusters of gestures. They will indicate more accurately the other negotiator's thoughts.

Hugs

Think about how people interact with each other when hugging. What significance can we draw from those nonverbal messages?

A man approaches a woman and he starts to hug her. She allows him to hug her in a full-body embrace. That's one sign of being more welcoming, receptive, and open. Let's also use the situation where the man begins to hug the woman and she's lukewarm about literally how close she allows him to get.

That's saying, "Hey buddy, there are boundaries and I want you to observe them."

Let's turn the situation around. The woman embraces the man with a full-body frontal hug and the man is a little lukewarm with his response. That implies, "You're a little bit too forward, and I'm a little apprehensive." You would think the exact opposite would be true in a male, but that signal is sending a specific message: "I feel a little discomfort as the result of you giving me that full frontal body hug."

Consider the next part of this. Let's say the male also is embracing the woman in a full frontal body hug. That could be conveying, "I accept you as an equal. You're not going to take over any of my territory. I will not take over any of yours. We're equals."

Concealment of Body Language

Knowing what you do about body language, you may make a deliberate attempt to conceal your reactions. Some people train themselves to mute their reactions. Health care professionals, as an example, are taught to maintain poker faces in the midst of some disturbing situations. That training can result in a pattern of controlling body language so as to not convey meaning to other people.

Similarly, skilled negotiators may make deliberate efforts to not react in any way. Imagine you detect that Bill is concealing, controlling, or muting his reactions in the midst of a negotiation. One approach is to confront him: "I'm just curious. You seem not to be emitting any emotion to anything I'm saying. Am I getting through to you?"

Watch how Bill reacts. He may lower his eyes and admit, "Yes, you're getting through to me." He still hasn't given you any real insight. But suppose he holds his head up, looks at you with a smile on his face, and acknowledges, "I'm listening very carefully to you." You might say something such as, "I'm glad you said that because I just wanted to make sure you're still here." "I'm definitely still here," Bill replies. See what the person does with his body language then.

Sometimes people conceal their body language because they know the person with whom they're negotiating will be able to decipher nonverbal signals that will be used in the negotiation. Even though they try to conceal their reactions, the body always attempts to be truthful. Our bodies will emit signals unbeknownst to us at times, even if we try to hold back signals. The body will naturally do things that are in alignment with what we believe to be true.

In addition to outright asking the other negotiator about the lack of body gestures, consider trying to change the whole atmosphere. If it's very somber, tell a joke and see what happens. Do something that may be considered outrageous. Watch the other negotiator's body language as you do so.

Low-Energy Body Language

A person who is either trying to conceal body language or displays low energy uses little facial expressions or body movements. Observe Bill for these clues:

- Bill's gestures are not aligned with what he is saying.
- He holds his arms and hands closer to his body.
- He does not make eye contact.
- His gestures lack force or emphasis.
- His voice is soft and slow.

Body language displays your reactions to the negotiator's strategies, offers, and counteroffers. By using it appropriately in a negotiation, you're also displaying to the other negotiator the degree of control you have.

There's a myth that the first person who speaks in a negotiation loses. That's not necessarily true. There are all kinds of variables that are involved in that scenario that dictate to what degree he who speaks first loses. One negotiator may be significantly better at reading body language or more astute when it comes to negotiation tactics. He may suspect the opponent thinks the person who speaks first loses—and may intentionally do just that.

Two negotiators were sitting across from one another and neither would say a word. That went on for several hours. One negotiator wrote on a piece of paper and slid it over to the other negotiator. It read, "You can speak and I'll still think that you're a winner." The other negotiator started laughing. You can do something to break the monotony. You can do something that will alter the perspective of what's occurring when someone is trying to conceal his body language gestures and see what he does with his body language then.

Controlling Hands

Imagine that you're sitting at the negotiation table and Bill is literally sitting on his hands such as not to give away hand gestures. What does that tell you about his body language? He's intentionally trying to conceal the hands so you don't get insight. You can ask something along the lines of, "I noticed the watch that you have on. It is very nice. May I take a look at it?" Bill will literally give you his arm or wrist. Now watch what he does next. Does he put his hand on the table? Do his hands go back to the seat?

There is a reason Bill is concealing his hands. You can just ask outright why: "Just out of curiosity, I am not seeing you use much body language. I wonder what is going through your mind. I'm always in a learning state."

If you place yourself for the moment in a subservient position, you can gain insight based on what the person does as he conceals his body language. What are his motives? For example, consider the physician who has to deliver bad news. You may notice that he'll put a hand on the shoulder of the person to whom he is speaking and say something like, "Don't worry about this. We're going to take good care of your father." There's that body language gesture again. He may say something along the lines of "He is unstable and I'm being straightforward with you. His prognosis is poor." Now if he were to say something like that, you would realize he is telling you something serious, and he even feels uncomfortable getting so close to you and the message that he's delivering.

Use your observation of the concealment of body language to evaluate the person's demeanor. Note how long the concealment actually lasts, what triggered it, and when it stops. Are your attempts successful to get Bill to be more open?

Exaggerated Body Language

Let's look at the other end of the spectrum when people are displaying either high energy or distress. Earlier I gave you the example of a person who jiggles a knee or a leg, which may be conveying a certain level of internal distress and trying to use that gesture to comfort himself. There are other signals that would indicate either distress or high energy and excitement.

When Bill is in distress, you will see exactly how agitated he is based on his speech patterns. Listen for rapid, pressured speech. The words tumble over each other. Bill does not pause between sentences. You can also discern the level of distress because you're watching his hand movements. They are synchronized with the energy he is projecting. Bill's hand movements generate even more energy as he speaks. Note what Bill does with his hands and watch for him to move his hands in synchrony with his speech. Imagine him holding his dominant hand perpendicular to the floor, moving it up and down with each word he says: "I—told—you—they—will—never—go—for—that—offer!" This body language shows Bill is in sync with what he is saying and the emotion he is feeling.

Suppose Bill says, "That's the worst deal I've ever heard in my life. I don't know where in the world you came up with those accusations and would even dare to make such an offer to me!" What does he convey with his body language? Is there synchrony between his statements, and hand and leg movements?

Bill says, "I hate this offer!" You'd expect to see him make a fist or move his hand downward as he literally "puts down the offer." He might spread his fingers and push the offer away with his hand to ward it off. These gestures are in synchrony with his feelings. The further away from the body the hand movement was, the greater he is displaying his dislike of the offer.

When Bill says, "I hate this" and does not move his hand down at the same time that he is ending on the word "this," you might question his statement. He may be using a ploy to exaggerate his response.

Bill could be truly appalled by the offer or he could also be showing high energy as a negotiating ploy to attempt to get you to change the terms of the offer.

With some negotiators, the display of distress appeals to their nurturing needs. Always remember no matter what people do, their motivation is to use a technique that is beneficial to their self-interest. If you're negotiating with someone who reveals this motivation, it may enhance your position to portray someone in distress. Be careful when you display distress. It may tempt an aggressive negotiator to attack you. Also, be on guard—the opponent could be using this display as a ploy.

Just like the display of distress can be used as an enhancer or detractor, the same is true when displaying high levels of energy. The calculation of when to display distress or high energy should first be considered in relation to the person with whom you're negotiating.

In Summary

Let's return to the situation at the beginning of this chapter when we found Bill talking with Sharma about buying his products. This is what Sharma observed in Bill:

- He was shifting in his seat every few minutes.
- His hands trembled.
- There was a thin sheen of perspiration on his face.

Sharma said, "Bill, I have a feeling that this sale means a lot to you." Although Bill denied this, he was immediately ready to make a deal. Sharma was successful because he focused on Bill's signs of distress and used that information in the negotiation.

The shifting in the seat indicated that Bill was actually uncomfortable. Your body always attempts to be truthful and will emit signals. In this case, with the sheen on Bill's forehead, his body was literally saying, "I'm getting hot" because he was having a physical reaction to the fact that he was lying and that came through. Bill's trembling hands showed he was nervous—his body reacted as he tried to deceive Sharma.

You can sense when a person is being honest or attempting to be dishonest. A good negotiator who knows how to use body language can attempt to control some of his gestures, but his body may reveal the truth of how he really feels. Just trying to prevent your hands from trembling can make them shake.

Bill gave away his position via his body language with the trembling of his hands, the sheen on his forehead, and the shifting in his seat to indicate that he was uncomfortable. Sharma's astuteness at reading body language led him to naturally make a lower offer. He could have raised the offer, but he sensed Bill really did need the business much more than he was indicating; Sharma got a better deal. Therein lies how being able to really understand and use body language can improve your position in any negotiation.

Chapter 2

✦ ✦ ✦ ✦ ✦ ✦ ✦ ✦ ✦ ✦ ✦ ✦

Microexpressions:
Catching One-Second Bursts of Emotion

Carla thought the interview was going well as she sat opposite Kyle. "I'd really like a job in this company," she thought. "It is perfect—it would allow me to work at home, use my skills, and do something creative. I know Kyle has been having trouble finding someone for this position. I wonder what the salary is."

Kyle concluded the interview by saying, "Carla, I think you would do well in this position. I'd like to be sure we are not wasting your time. If I offer you this position, do you have a salary in mind?" Carla said, "Yes, I'd like $60,000 a year." Kyle's eyes widened in shock. Carla caught his look and said, "Of course, that is negotiable." Kyle thought, "I never dreamed I could get her at such a low price! I would have offered $100,000." He pretended to think about this, and replied, "The best we can do is $55,000." Carla responded, "Perfect. I will take it."

Microexpressions Defined

Carla misinterpreted Kyle's nonverbal body language, a mistake that cost her $45,000 a year. A form of body language, microexpressions are unfiltered displays of emotion that occur in less than 1 second. They reveal the other negotiator's mind-set, which you can use to strengthen your position *if* you correctly decode them. Microexpressions give you a momentary glimpse into someone's mind. Since your opponent's brain does not have the opportunity to interrupt the display before it's made, the microexpression discloses the person's real thoughts, emotions, and feelings. Body language can give us away based on the non-verbal signals we send in the form of microexpressions. Now there's a great importance to microexpressions for just that reason. You are not thinking about how you should respond.

Microexpressions last for no more than a second, and some people say three-quarters of a second, the time that it takes to blink your eye.

In the story above, Carla misinterpreted the body language signal she sensed from Kyle. One of the things she should have been much more aware of was what the signal she sensed *really* meant. She accurately determined it was surprise Kyle communicated. It meant that he was pleasantly surprised at what she said since she had underestimated what he was prepared to pay her. He displayed surprise simply because he was caught off guard. That's what surprise will do to you a lot of times. Without thinking, you will communicate a truthful microexpression.

Had Carla taken the time to ask probing questions as a good negotiator should always do about what she sensed, she would have had better insight into what that expression meant. She then could have reshaped her perspective based on the number she gave.

As you read this chapter, you will discover how microexpressions come about, the seven universal microexpressions that are generic to everybody in the world, and why they are so important to understand.

Seven Universal Microexpressions

The seven microexpressions that are generic to everyone are fear, anger, disgust, surprise, contempt, sadness, and happiness. The microexpressions are universal in that cultures all over the world share in these expressions.

Fear

I've done demonstrations to elicit a startle or fear reaction. I will bring someone up on stage during my presentation. I will ask him if he knows he is in a safe environment. He'll say, "Yes." I'll respond, "Okay, so you know nobody is out to harm you," which serves as confirmation for the fact that he is in a safe environment. He will agree. I will reiterate: "You know you're in a safe environment and you know nobody is out to harm you." Then I'll scream. Inevitably he will jump, duck, or display fear. Even though he knows he is in a safe environment and no one is out to harm him, the scream made him experience fear.

My experiment shows he was displaying not only the micro-expressions associated with fear but also an innate reaction. Fear is one of the protective mechanisms.

I know one particular individual who considered himself to be an extreme daredevil. He loved to hike very close to the edge of a cliff. He wanted the rush, the thrills. "My body will never allow me to get too close to the edge," he told me. That is the body's way of protecting itself. It's the same thing with micro-expressions, which are ways to display your inner emotions as you protect yourself.

Fear is usually denoted when you raise your eyebrows, open your eyes widely, and slightly stretch or open your lips. Your bottom lip protrudes downward.

When we are fearful of something the reason the eyes widen is because we want to take in as much of the environment as we possibly can. In so doing we are able to make decisions based on everything we're able to glean so we can determine what we should do next.

Anger

An angry person has her eyebrows down and together. You will see her glaring, narrowing her lips, and flaring her nostrils. You get the message that she is literally glaring at you; she is not happy with what you have done, said, or some other reason.

Keep in mind that her eyebrows would be raised if she sensed fear and lowered when angry. Therein lies the slight way you can differentiate between the two microexpressions.

Disgust

Disgust is conveyed by lifting the upper lip, almost like if your opponent smelled something foul and he is wrinkling his nose from it. Now, therein lies an easy way to detect disgust. His microexpression displays he does not like what he is hearing or sensing.

Julie Robbins sat next to a physician, Peter Auckland. Peter was a very friendly guy and he had an open questioning, appreciative look on his face when Julie said she was a nurse. She then explained she previously had a business working with medical malpractice attorneys. As Julie said that, she watched his face. She saw him wrinkle his nose; she watched the friendly expression in his eyes dissolve. Peter's smile disappeared. He looked extremely stern. Julie explained that she sold her business and no longer worked with attorneys. Peter's smile came back; his nose smoothed out and the light came back in his eyes.

Julie wondered about the cluster of expressions she saw and realized Peter's microexpression displayed his attitude toward somebody who helped attorneys.

Surprise

Surprise is conveyed with raised eyebrows, wide eyes, and open mouth. Recall just reading that you can convey fear with raised eyebrows and wide eyes. Fear and surprise have that in common. The open mouth does not necessarily have to be a part of surprise, but you will usually see the raised eyebrows and the wide eyes.

How do you differentiate between the microexpressions of fear and surprise? You watch for more signals when you are not sure what your opponent is displaying. Look for clusters of expressions to validate what you are seeing.

Contempt

Contempt is communicated by a sneer: The opponent raises one corner of her lip on one side of her face. Remember these expressions last for less than a second, so you have to be very observant to note exactly what is occurring. Then confirm what has just happened by asking probing questions.

Sadness

With sadness the upper eyelids appear to be drooping. The eyes are unfocused. The lips are slightly turned down and you will hear a change in tone. Your nonverbal microexpression and your tone combine to project sadness.

Here is another tip for training yourself to recognize microexpressions. Act the way you would normally act if you are angry. Act the way you would normally act if you were disgusted with something. Act the way you would act if you were surprised by something, and the same thing is true with sadness. If you're sad, take note of your facial expressions in order to become more astute at detecting microexpressions.

Happiness

Last, let's look at happiness. A happy person has a wide-eyed expression—smiled, elevated cheeks, and wide eyes. You're displaying the gaiety you are feeling, perhaps at the end of a successful negotiation.

Interpreting Microexpressions during Negotiations

Those are some of the traits associated with being able to detect the seven universal microexpressions. There are other gestures that might be microexpressions based on the length of time the gesture is displayed.

For example, if I say to you, "This offer is going to really make you feel good," you might touch your stomach. Your hand stays there for less than a second. That might be a microexpression that you displayed, meaning, "I am so pleased to hear that. Boy, this is going to make me feel good." You'd also be kinesthetically conveying your sentiments, which would give the opposing negotiator insight as to how something might be affecting you emotionally.

Microexpressions give you insight during a negotiation. Your strategy depends on accurately reading them so you don't make the mistake that Carla made by leaving so much more than she could have had on the negotiation table.

Look at how microexpressions affected a purchase. David Cowen stared at Nancy Winters as he made an offer to purchase her car. Her eyes widened, her cheeks rose, and she smiled. David thought, "I think she is pleasantly surprised with the offer that I just made. I wonder if I named a higher number than she expected. David said, "You know what, I just sensed something. Can you please tell me what it was that I just saw a moment ago?"

Nancy replied, "I don't know. What did you see?"

David responded, "I saw a little sense of happiness, a broad smile on your face. I was just curious. What were you feeling at that moment?"

"Oh, nothing; I was just thinking to myself that this negotiation is going well," Nancy said.

"Okay. *Why* did you think that in that moment?" David queried.

David is probing to not only understand the microexpression that he sensed, but also why he sensed it and how important it was. This type of probing helps you validate the meaning of what you observed.

Microexpressions as Body Language

Body language consists of both verbal and nonverbal communication. There are ways that we can say something like "I love you," and the same words can have different connotations based on our intonation. That becomes a verbal form of body language. The body language that's associated with our words colors our communication. Microexpressions add extra meaning and insight into your opponent's thought processes.

Your body always attempts to be truthful. When it emits a microexpression, what it's really doing is letting you know something happened. Either I was fearful or angry about something that happened or I was disgusted. I was surprised or felt contempt. I feel sad or happy. From a microexpression perspective, those are a person's reality as of the moment that person emits those signals.

A very savvy negotiator can feign a microexpression. Now that may sound contrary to what I said a moment ago about microexpressions being real. Yes, they are real 99.9% of the time, but I can feign surprise if I control my microexpressions based on the offer that you made. A lot of people try to feign anger but may not effectively use the cluster of expressions associated with anger: the eyebrows down together, eyes glaring, narrowing of the lips, and the nostrils flaring.

What Causes Microexpressions?

People display microexpressions because it's a part of our DNA. Centuries ago when we were hunters if we saw something that caused us to experience fear we instantly just raised our eyebrows and opened our eyes wider. We wanted to see more of what might possibly harm us. Our reactions evolved to help us adapt.

Our nervous system responds to threats with a fight or flight reaction, a complex series of chemicals called neurotransmitters that help us respond.

Microexpressions help to protect us. There are times when we are about to eat something and discover it has spoiled. We would display the microexpression of disgust by scrunching up our nose and lifting the upper lip. Our face reveals that something is not exactly the way it should be; that's a self-protective mechanism. We displayed that microexpression just naturally because something doesn't smell right to us.

Rebecca Marginelli was negotiating with Robert Warner and Dale Acuff. They were sitting in a noisy restaurant. Rebecca sat next to Robert, and Dale sat across the table from Rebecca. Robert was a very large man who had an extremely loud voice. He was enthusiastically describing the value of his company's services and trying to convince Rebecca to buy them. Robert was waving his arms around and shouting.

Rebecca recoiled from Robert: She leaned as far away as possible to the point that if she had leaned any further she would have fallen off her chair. As she leaned she also put her hand up, covering the ear closest to Robert. Watching Rebecca's body language, Dale had a microexpression of intense amusement. He then became noticeably warmer to Rebecca as the conversation went on.

From a negotiation perspective, Rebecca realized that Dale's allegiance to Robert had undergone a subtle shift. He was not "feeling" Robert, meaning he was not in the same mind-set as Robert. When he saw Rebecca's body language of pulling away and putting a hand up to cover her ear, he knew Rebecca and he were aligned in their feelings toward Robert's loudness. This communication took place even though Dale and Rebecca had not said a word to one another. He was able to convey this in his microexpression.

Robert should have also been much more aware of the body language that Dale and Rebecca were displaying. Had he been aware of the body language and microexpressions, he might have realized that he needed to tone his voice down.

Bigger people need to be very aware of the extra projection their size has in any environment when they are negotiating.

There are times when big people will be perceived to be more aggressive simply because of their size. People start making assumptions based on what they've experienced in the past even though Robert might not have done anything aggressive. In this case, Robert's loudness might have confirmed that opinion.

Dale might have thought to himself, "Wow, at least I'm not the only one that thinks this guy may be a jerk. He's definitely talking too loud." Rebecca wanted to make Dale into an ally. She decided to play on her suspicion that Robert's behavior was alienating Dale. During the negotiation, she looked at Dale out of the corner of her eye from time to time and just nodded her head to convey, "Oh, there he goes again, but you and I understand what's going on." This shows how, through microexpressions, you can communicate among yourselves as to how in sync you might be with the progress of a negotiation.

Impact of Microexpressions on Negotiation

You make an offer during a negotiation and notice your opponent raises his eyebrows, leans away from you, and protrudes his lower lip. "He does not like my offer," you think. You decide not to question your opponent, but instead you continue with your plan. As you talk, you watch his face. He raises one side of his lip; you recognize he is contemptuous and fearful about what you are saying. "How should I revise my strategy?" you wonder. "What should I do to sweeten the deal? Should I back off on one of the points I am trying to win?"

Microexpressions have a profound impact on the negotiation process. The better any negotiator is at accurately detecting microexpressions, the greater the success in negotiating with offers and counter offers.

Why Carla lost $45,000

I started the chapter describing Carla's and Kyle's negotiation. When Kyle's eyes widened in shock, Carla misinterpreted that signal and immediately backed off from her salary demand by saying the money she was asking for was negotiable. Carla could have improved her perspective by understanding the microexpressions that Kyle was displaying. It's just good negotiation sense to probe when you're not sure of what you're sensing in any negotiation. False steps will color the rest of the negotiation.

Carla should have probed to identify what she sensed. She may not have known it was surprise she was observing, but she was astute enough to detect something. A more favorable negotiation would have resulted if she thought, "If I'm not sure of what I'm sensing, I need to find out what it is before making an offer." By literally moving forward without comprehending the meaning of Kyle's microexpression, she cheated herself out of $45,000 a year. Had she taken the time to learn about microexpressions ahead of time, she would have been in a much better position to negotiate with Kyle.

Even though Carla did not know about microexpressions, she could have acted on her feeling of unease and asked herself, "What did I just experience?" Remember, as a good negotiator you never ever want to negotiate unless you're prepared. When you're in a negotiation and your opponent uses an unexpected tactical strategy, back off. Carla violated that particular protocol.

Now let's take a step aside. I don't care how good a negotiator you are, there are times depending upon circumstances that you will negotiate knowing that you should not. I had an associate who was affected by two unpleasant experiences that affected his ability to negotiate. Not even fully thinking about his mental state, he entered into a third negotiation and realized afterwards he just caved in. He did so simply because of his mind-set. Carla should have been more aware that her desire for the job put her at risk for an unfavorable deal. Her state of mind made her vulnerable. That's why it's so important to call a time-out when you're not sure of where it is that you're going. Yet it happens to the best of us at times that we don't call a time-out simply because we're just not as aware as we should be.

There's another aspect of this situation that is troubling. Kyle asked Carla, "What is your salary requirement?" Carla gave a number of $60,000 a year. Kyle was prepared to spend at least $100,000 a year to bring her into the company. Clearly, Carla put herself at a disadvantage even before she misinterpreted the microexpression. What could Carla have done when she was asked the question, "What is your salary requirement?" She should have had background information about standard salary ranges in the industry and the importance Kyle placed on hiring her. Kyle already said that he thought that she was a good fit. That is a closing signal, in sales terms, which Carla should have detected to what degree Kyle liked her and needed her skills for the company.

Suppose Carla did research on typical salaries for the position for which she interviewed. Let's say she gathered data that showed for the particular function that she would be performing, the salary range was between $75,000 and $125,000. She then could have bracketed her expectations for her salary requirements before entering into the negotiation. Second, after knowing the range was between $75,000 and $125,000, she realized that the ceiling for the position was $125,000 and the floor was $75,000. She labeled the midrange as $100,000. Prepared with this knowledge, Carla entered into the negotiation with Kyle. When asked, "What are your salary requirements?" she said, "I did some research and found that the range is between $100,000 and $125,000 for people who accept the jobs in this industry."

Did Carla bend the truth? It depends on your perspective. She quoted a range for a strategic purpose, knowing she had some flexibility.

The point is that there are times when you never want to give the first number. People have said many times that "he who gives the first number is the loser in the negotiation." I temper that with "not necessarily so" because there are other mitigating circumstances. The better of the two negotiators may be able to overcome whatever obstacles may come up in a negotiation. She is better prepared to negotiate to the degree that one negotiator also has a plan in place based on whenever mitigating circumstances occur.

Had Carla gathered the data she needed, she would have been much more prepared to negotiate with Kyle from more of an equal perspective.

Improving Your Position with Microexpressions

Effective interpretation of microexpressions involves taking the opportunity to reflect on what you are sensing in your opponent and questioning its accuracy. This reflection takes place in microseconds, in the heat of a discussion, and requires you to think on your feet to reshape your negotiation offer.

Let's say also that instead of Kyle being prepared to offer Carla $100,000, that he was ready to offer her $125,000. Carla knows this is the ceiling for the position. She would love to accept $125,000 as her salary. In our new scenario, Kyle says, "I'm willing to give you $125,000 for this job." Carla deliberately drops her eyes and looks sad.

Carla's preparation led her to realize no matter how good that first offer was she was going to feign a microexpression, and she did that for no more than a second that it took to occur. If by chance Kyle did not pick that up, she could then back away as though she was fearful. Her eyebrows were raised, her bottom lip protruding downward, and her lips slightly have stretched apart. Carla feigned these emotions to convey at a microexpression level to Kyle, "Your offer is just not good enough."

Another strategy to adopt would be not to say anything to Kyle about his salary offer. Silence often has a great impact; there are many different ways to use microexpressions. Even when feigning microexpressions you have to be aware your opponent may ask you probing questions to determine the meaning of your microexpression. Be prepared to answer those questions.

I have shared what Carla should have done to gather research and plan the negotiation. She should also take into account what microexpressions Kyle might display, when he might display them, and why he might display them. When Carla saw them as she predicted, she could use that knowledge to gauge how she was progressing in the negotiation. She would have valuable feedback about where her positions were succeeding at that point.

The Absence of Microexpressions

Feigning microexpressions involves a deliberate projection of an emotion that's contrary to the way that you might be feeling. Is it really possible to be completely opaque or have a wooden face and not react at all? We refer to these individuals as "poker faced" or inscrutable.

Being poker faced is not our typical state. Suppose somebody walks up in back of you where you can't see and suddenly makes a loud sound or touches you. You're going to react. This is a reflex rooted in our infancy. We are born fearing loud noises and falling. Neonatologists take into their arms a newborn just minutes old. The physician quickly moves his arms down. The baby will react based on an innate fear of falling. The doctors clap their hands near the baby's ear and watch the baby jump.

Our reflexes and reactions are so innate that when you hide what you are feeling, you can become conspicuous. Your opponent knows it is not natural to sit through a negotiation for an extended period without displaying emotions. A savvy opponent will gain insight from watching you. "What is she hiding?" he may wonder. "What are her true feelings? What is she trying to gain by keeping a poker face?"

I recall the time I sat in a negotiation with a guy who steepled his hands, with his palms together and fingers pointing upward. This body language showed authority, designed to display that he was very confident and knew what he was doing. We sat like that for 45 minutes. The whole time we sat in that negotiation he maintained his steepled hands. Throughout that time I actually mimicked him by steepling my hands. I changed my pose to see if he would follow and he never did.

After the negotiation we developed a closer relationship. "Why did you maintain that body language?" I inquired. He snickered, "I wanted to see what you would do because I figured you knew what I was actually doing."

We laughed later because both of us understood each other's actions. I knew also he was feigning that gesture. It's the same thing with microexpressions or any way that you use your body language to convey your sentiments. If you hold a body language display too long, more than likely it's not genuine. Your opponent may realize you are trying to send a signal that's not truly the way you feel.

Carla's Choices for Strategies

Carla made some obvious errors by not being prepared with homework on the typical salary range and also misinterpreting the microexpression of Kyle. Once she gave her salary number, she could have strengthened her position. What that means is that in Carla's case, she should have negotiated with Kyle after she gave a salary number to find out what Kyle had in mind. Here's what could have occurred:

Kyle: "What is your salary requirement?"

Carla: "$60,000. What do you have in mind?"

Kyle: "I'm not really sure I had a real number in mind." Kyle shrugged his shoulders and glanced away from her as he talked. These gestures may not have connoted a microexpression, but by the fact that he lost eye contact indicated he was not being completely forthright.

Watching his body language, Carla probed: "You didn't really have a number in mind?"

Notice how Carla asked that question. She allowed her voice to rise at the end of the sentence. That's something else to take note of too, because raising the voice always puts a statement in the form of a question.

Carla: "Would $300,000 be satisfactory?"

Although Kyle said that he didn't have a salary in mind, now Carla could have stretched even further to $200,000. By going above whatever the bracket Carla forced Kyle to respond.

Kyle: "I can't offer above $110,000."

Carla: "What number can you offer? $100,000?"

Kyle: "No, I'm not sure if I can offer $100,000."

Carla: "Why? It's below $110,000."

Carla observes Kyle's body language. One side of his lip is raised ever so slightly for a moment. What he's now doing is displaying contempt for the questioning that Carla is putting him under, and he's starting to feel a little uneasy.

This is the danger in agreeing on a dollar amount you're going to engage in with someone and then going back and trying to renegotiate it.

Carla: "I know I said $60,000, but you know I think what would be fair would be more of $100,000 or somewhere in that range."

Kyle: "Okay, we'll make it $100,000. You are a good fit for the job. We can offer that salary." In the back of his mind, Kyle is always going to think, "She said $60,000 and she went to $100,000. I'll keep that thought in the back of my mind that somewhere down the line I'm going to make myself whole."

Carla took a risk of not only ruining the relationship that she and Kyle were starting, but at the same time she showed that she might try to take advantage of the situation. Kyle may think to himself that he has to be harder when dealing with her in the future. There are ramifications to how you position yourself in a negotiation while at the same time understanding the trap of acquiescing too fast or giving a number too quickly.

Had Carla been much more astute, she would have taken the time to find out the salary range and not be overly exuberant about the fact that she had a job offer. Instead, she should have said, "I have a job offer. Let's make sure I get fairly compensated for it."

Negotiating for Benefits

One of the negotiation principles is that you can accept a lower number for one part of a deal but enhance your total compensation with other features. Carla had a choice of saying she would accept $55,000 as a salary, but she also wanted four weeks of paid vacation, profit sharing, fully paid health insurance, and a company car. In other words, Carla could have layered on additional forms of compensation that meant something to her even though they did not match the income she just unknowingly lost.

For Carla to request these benefits, she needed to understand there was more on the table—more to be obtained. Carla did not even probe to find out if she could get more. One of the things that she sensed was surprise, which made her lower her demand. Kyle understood that her offer was more than likely not her firmest number when he went below that to $55,000. He took even more away from her than she otherwise could have had. She more than likely accepted the $55,000 too quickly.

Consider another strategy Carla could have used. She stated her salary demand was $60,000 and caught a microexpression on Kyle's face that looked like surprise. Suppose when Carla saw the expression of surprise on Kyle's face, she probed, "What did I just sense?" Kyle responded, "I don't know. You were the one that felt it, so you tell me." Note how Kyle was putting Carla into a corner to push her to probe.

Carla retorted, "I thought I sensed you were surprised." He said, "I was." As a negotiation strategy, Carla wanted Kyle to reveal why he was surprised. She has to get him to be honest and not deflect her inquiry. Now she has a little more input to work with. She questioned, "Why were you surprised?" Kyle looks pensive, trying to figure out how to avoid sharing his shock at her low number. After Carla sits in silence waiting for him to answer, Kyle reveals, "I thought your salary require-ments would have been a little higher." This answer permits Carla to consider asking for a higher salary or tacking on the benefits to raise her compensation.

Here's another thing to contemplate. If the salary range was bracketed as I indicated earlier of $75,000 to $125,000, the benefits would add up to about 25%. Salary plus additional benefits would be 25% more of whatever salary she was get-ting. Suppose Carla found out through research she did ahead of time the bracket was $75,000 to $125,000 and she settled for $75,000. The benefits would not have added up to reach the $100,000 Kyle had in mind.

Deciphering Microexpressions in a Cultural Context

A savvy negotiator will learn how to recognize microexpressions and the moods they convey. Earlier in the chapter I stressed you should think about the different mind-sets you put yourself in when you are sad, fearful, or angry. Note how you really feel at such times. Draw on that knowledge when you're watching other individuals. Train yourself to watch how others display emotions through microexpressions. In so noting you will become more astute at recognizing the genuineness of microexpressions.

The better you become at deciphering microexpressions, the better you will become as a negotiator simply because you'll have so much additional insight based on the way your opponent uses his body and reveals his emotions through microexpressions. Use this knowledge to guide you in modifying or sweetening your position or taking something away.

Acute observation will help you get more insight about when you sense microexpressions. In addition, by reading this book you'll also gain a lot of value about microexpressions and their meaning and the impact they have on the overall flow of body language during a negotiation.

Astute negotiators do their homework on the cultural background of their opponent. You need to understand the culture of others when you negotiate with them. For example, you may encounter Japanese people who appear overtly polite, with a lot of bowing and displays of deference. The Japanese value proper decorum and not alienating people; they may project an impression of being in agreement even if they do not feel that way.

I think someone once said the word "no" is not in the Japanese vocabulary. I don't know to what degree that is true. What may happen is in the Japanese society, you will hear "yes." Although you think while you're negotiating you have a deal, in reality what they're saying is "Yes, we agree to disagree" or "Yes, we'll take this to the next stage." Even when you think you have a negotiated deal, in the Japanese society that means you have negotiated it to the first phase and now it's time for the second phase.

You always have to understand your opponents' culture when you are trying to assess to what degree they may be displaying microexpressions or holding back their natural expressions simply because it's part of their society to not display anger, as an example.

Now, here's a way to test this. Be careful about how you do this. If you knew in their culture they did not display anger in public, you could intentionally do something to anger them. Watch to see to what degree they display either contempt, disgust, fear, or anger. You will at least know that there is a button you can push later if you chose to do so. This is a common tactic.

I'll give you another quick example. At the end of World War II, the Japanese were not ready to come to the negotiation table because they wanted their emperor to have the same powers and status he had prior to the war. That was a point of contention, because the United States took the position Japan had to unconditionally surrender.

In any negotiation you have to take into consideration who's not at the negotiation table. In this situation, the Russians had also started encroaching upon Japan. The Japanese were concerned about what would occur if the Russians got involved in the negotiation process. Even more so was the United States's concern as to what would happen if Russia became involved. Thus, the United States backed off from the requirement for an unconditional statement of surrender and allowed the emperor to have some ceremonial powers.

Understand the culture and to what degree microexpressions may play a role. Remember that microexpressions are emotional displays lasting for less than a second. Even though they're taught in the Japanese culture to not display anger in public, you can catch a glimpse of it if you have done something to really anger them and you're astute enough to catch it.

My colleague inadvertently infuriated a female Japanese tour guide by being 5 minutes late coming back to the tour bus after being separated from her group of friends. The tour guide told my colleague in clear and distinct words that she was supposed to be back at 10:00 and 10:05 A.M. was not acceptable. A repeat infraction would result in her entire group being removed from the bus and left behind. Punctuality is highly prized in the Japanese culture. My colleague worked out a plan with her group that they would not allow themselves to be separated.

A month later my colleague was on a Caribbean tour that was supposed to leave at 9 A.M. They were on "island time" and waited for an hour in the sunshine for a guest who *might* be coming on the tour. Note the difference between the cultures related to time.

In South America many years ago, I had the opportunity to travel to Venezuela on a project. I was told ahead of time to understand that the culture there is different. If someone says to you, "I'll have it by Tuesday," they may mean "I'll have it by Thursday, Friday, Monday, or maybe Tuesday of the following week." Thus, don't get upset if you go to a restaurant and you don't get the quick service that you would experience in the United States. It's a slower pace, a different environment, and thus the reason you always have to understand the environment you are in and how culture affects microexpressions, body language, and negotiation tactics.

In Summary

To the degree you can become astute at accurately sensing, reading, and detecting microexpressions, you can enhance your negotiation abilities. It gives you a huge advantage at the negotiation table. Practice observing microexpressions and interpreting their meaning.

Public places are good settings for practice. For example, you can look at people in the airport and sometimes you can just tell what they are experiencing by the expressions on their faces. There have been times when I've walked up to someone in an airport, introduced myself, and told them that I was a body language expert. I told them what I sensed and that I was trying to confirm my conclusions. I have found people respond to me by confirming my conclusions and offering explanations. Try this exercise to add to the repertoire of knowledge that you build up. To the degree you get very good at it, you become a better negotiator.

Chapter 3

✦ ✦ ✦ ✦ ✦ ✦ ✦ ✦ ✦ ✦ ✦

Primers: *Preparing for the Emotional Game*

Jessica prepared the conference room for the negotiation. She ordered fresh flowers to create an impression of opulence. She hid the plastic cups. Crystal glasses rested on a sideboard. Jessica turned down the lighting to increase the sense of exclusivity. She asked her assistant to hold all calls during the meeting. Before the other negotiator arrived, Jessica rehearsed how she would start the negotiation and the main points she wanted to make. Just before the elevator chimed the arrival of her guests, her eyes swept the room. "Let the games begin," she thought, "I am ready."

Targets for Priming

This chapter relates to priming: preparing for the emotional game. Preparation involves planning how you will react in a negotiation and anticipating what the other negotiator will feel and do. Plan your own body language as well as what type of body language signals you will seek to provoke from the other negotiator. Think about how you're going to react and how you will keep the negotiation flowing toward your objectives. Priming does not occur exclusively before a negotiation begins; as you will learn, you may use priming during a negotiation in response to what takes place.

Priming encompasses controlling the physical environment, your opponent, those not at the negotiation table, and yourself.

Priming the environment

I started this chapter by describing how Jessica deliberately primed the environment through lighting and objects to project a certain atmosphere and provoke reactions from the other negotiator. Negotiators may use a variety of subliminal tactics to affect the environment. As an example, you can increase discomfort by setting the room temperature lower or higher than comfortable.

Stephen Woodruff watched the reactions of Bonnie Mallick as she entered the board room. Because the negotiation took place in his environment, he had control of the room's temperature. The thermostat was outside the room. Prior to the meeting, he reduced the room temperature as a subtle method of priming her for a difficult negotiation. "It's a little chilly in here," she said as she buttoned her suit jacket. Bonnie was oblivious to the fact that Stephen deliberately turned down the temperature. Stephen replied, "I'll make it a little more comfortable for you." Watch how these subliminal messages are repeated during the negotiation. Stephen made an offer to Bonnie that she found unacceptable. She responded, "That offer is making it a little chilly in here." Subliminally, she just referred back to the level of discomfort that she was feeling.

Stephen heard her discomfort and inquired, "Why do you say that?" Giving Stephen an annoyed look, Bonnie retorted, "I need a more comfortable offer." Stephen hid a smile as he realized his priming worked. He had anchored the negotiation around the concept of discomfort, using words that tied back to her perspective.

As the negotiation progressed, Stephen asked for some significant concessions from Bonnie. He sent a text message to his associate that said, "Turn down the thermostat." Any time Bonnie balked at Stephen's terms, Stephen texted his associate to turn down the temperature. Bonnie finally capitulated: "Fine, I agree to what you are proposing. I need to get out of here and get more comfortable."

Stephen sent one final text message: "All is good. Raise the temperature." By turning the temperature back up, Stephen rewarded Bonnie for giving in.

Priming your adversary

The more you know about the other negotiator, the easier it is to incorporate that knowledge into your priming.

- Is she an aggressive person when she negotiates?
- Is she a timid individual when she negotiates?
- To what degree might you be able to make her more timid based on the fact that she needs the deal that you're offering her?
- To what degree might she flinch as a tactic using body language gestures to send the nonverbal message that you've come too close to the edge and are causing her to back away from the negotiation offer?

The more insight you have about the motivation, strategies, and body language gestures that she will use, the better equipped you will be to understand how you can alter her perspective based on how you use your body language. Should you display aggression by leaning too close to her and cause her to weaken or be more receptive to accepting your counteroffer? Or is she the type of individual that if you lean too close to her she'll lean right back into you and instead of weakening, she becomes aggressive? All of those aspects are what you need to know about the other negotiator so that you can plan appropriately and thus understand what priming techniques you might use in the negotiation.

Consider what you know about your opponent. Ask yourself:

- What triggers might you be able to use to agitate or calm the individual?
- What body language will you use to add emphasis to or soften what you are saying?
- What pressures might you apply to wear the other negotiator down or to pick her up?
- What persona are you going to project? Will you be the nice guy or harsh?

Part of priming is considering how you can increase the other person's receptivity to the negotiation. For example, your first question on the phone when you call your opponent is, "Is this a good time to talk?" What does that question accomplish? Based on what you know of the other negotiator, you recognize that he is a powerful person who is used to being treated with deference. Your question about the timing of the discussion conveys that you are considerate and respectful.

You could also choose not to ask that question. Starting a negotiation without asking if the person is ready to talk could set the tone that you are an aggressive negotiator. "We need to get this deal done, and I don't have time to waste; let's do it now." You are taking control.

Take into consideration the type of individual that you're speaking to and how you expect him to react. Do you want to disarm a powerful person by being solicitous? Or do you want to control a weaker adversary?

What stimuli will you use throughout the negotiation to make the opponent feel a certain way? Plan how you will use those reactions to your advantage. Priming is akin to getting inside of the other negotiator's mind-set and then determining how you might shift that mind-set to your advantage.

Your body language and words prime the other negotiator. Consider what body language gestures would best suit the message that you want to convey. For example, you could say with a smile on your face, "Don't worry about it. I'm going to make sure you are 100% satisfied with this deal. You will have nothing to fear from it." My voice conveys compassion and is consistent with my body language. Contrast that same sentence said while you shake your head and look doubtful. When confronted with a conflict between your body language and your words, your opponent is likely to react to your body language and become wary.

Offering food or drink is a common way to prime the other negotiator. Robert and Samantha are buying their first home together. They are ready to make an offer and are sitting with their realtor in the living room of the owner, Lorna. She asks, "Would you like anything to drink? Is there anything I can do to make you comfortable?" Lorna is trying to make the couple feel at home and more comfortable. The priming message is, "This is the right environment for you to be in. I'm going to make you feel comfortable." What does that say subliminally? You are going to feel right at home. You should engage in this deal.

Lorna smiles and reaches over and touches the back of Robert's hand while she says, "You will be at home here." The smile goes a long way. She's saying, "Let me show you how comforting this environment is going to be." Lorna watches Robert's reaction. As soon as she withdrew her hand, Robert pulled his hand away and hid it in his pocket.

That body language signal says, "Wait a minute; not so fast, Lorna. We just started talking, so let's not move too quickly." Therein lies a signal that told Lorna she had to do a little more work to convince this prospective buyer that this is the right environment. Robert is saying just with that one little gesture, "Don't come so close to me so fast."

Lorna shook her head as she realized her mistake. "I should have planned that better," she thought. "He still looks ill at ease and Samantha is watching him, looking for a signal as to how he should behave." Lorna asked them, "What can I get for you that will make you comfortable?" Samantha declined a drink. As Robert replied, "orange juice," Lorna noted he avoided eye contact and looked around the living room.

Lorna thought, "I wonder if he is thinking about what it would be like to live here?" "The sunsets are beautiful from the deck—the sky fills this room with golden light," she told them. She watched Robert and Samantha grin and relax back into the sofa.

Priming someone else on your team

Not only do you need to know about the other negotiator so that you can prime for the event appropriately as Jessica did with the flowers and the crystal glasses as opposed to the plastic cups, but you also need to know who is not at the negotiation table. From a priming perspective, always consider who will be at the negotiation table and who will not be there. Consider the impact of absent negotiators (silent stakeholders) and the priming tactics you might apply to influence them. As an example, you might consider making an offer or counteroffer that is extremely appealing tied to a time constraint to which the negotiator at the table cannot commit. Thus, she'd have to contact the power negotiator who is not at the table. By gaining such insight, you flush out the real power and you know to what degree the person at the table can negotiate. The person with whom you are really interacting with may be nothing more than a shill. If that's the case, she then becomes a puppet. She's there to find out your position. Your body language will convey your messages, seriousness, sincerity, and flexibility.

Remember, when you're negotiating, the more information you have, the more options you can use.

Heidi Crawford glanced down at the word she wrote on the pad by her side: "Desperate." Carlo Antonio sat across from her, quivering with anxiety. Carlo asked, "Are we ready to make a deal?" Recognizing that Carlo was putting up a front of bravado, although clearly in need of completing this deal, Heidi said, "I have to call my boss." She excused herself and went out in the hall and spoke to her boss. "Sarah, here's the situation. Carlo says he wants to sell his consulting services for $10,000 a year. I think we can get him down to $7,500. It is time for you to come in." Note that Heidi could have asked for a concession from Carlo and then called Sarah. If she'd done so and Carlo denied Heidi's request, Heidi and Sarah could have played a game of good cop/bad cop, which could have brought more pressure upon Carlo.

Priming yourself

Let me take this a step further. Priming includes understanding your motivations for the negotiation, your mood, and your vulnerabilities.

Penny glanced up at Crystal, who stood in the threshold of her office. "Luke Fort is on the phone. He just got his invoice for our services, and he sounds really angry." Penny groaned. Tired from not getting much sleep and feeling sluggish, Penny did not want to deal with an irate client. She took a deep sigh and said, "Please tell him I am involved in something right now and I will call him back in 10 minutes." Shrugging on her coat, Penny walked out into the cold winter air. After pacing in front of her office for 10 minutes, she felt ready to speak to Luke about his concerns.

It is critical that you be aware of how much energy you have before you begin a negotiation. Priming yourself involves recognizing the hampering role of stress, fatigue, or preoccupation and taking steps to sharpen your focus.

Measuring the Effectiveness of Priming

Although you enter a negotiation with expectations about what will happen, there are often unpredictable factors that affect a negotiation. What kinds of cues can you pick up in the process of the negotiation that will give you feedback on whether the priming has been effective?

Bud Lorenzo felt himself getting angry at the man sitting next to him. Prior to their meeting, Brian told Bud that he was ready to close the deal. All they had to do was sign the papers. But the discussion was not going well. Bud saw the deal slipping away, so he decided to reveal some of his emotion. He displayed his aggression by leaning close to Brian as they talked. What Bud expected Brian to do was to lean to the opposite side to get further away from Bud.

Instead, Brian did not withdraw; he leaned toward Bud. "That did not work," thought Bud. "I have to change my tactics." Bud became more strident and loudly exclaimed, "I don't think that's appropriate. That offer you have on the table does not fit with what we had discussed before." Bud was upping the game. "From what I know of this guy, I think he is going to back off," thought Bud. Brian put his hand on Bud's forearm and said, "Okay, let's rethink that." Brian's body language said, "I need to placate you. I miscalculated."

Consider what will also make someone feel as though he is in a more emotionally heated environment than is comfortable. Calculate to what degree that person will go in order to experience more comfort. These aspects can be observed during a negotiation and thus the reason you also need to know how you're going to react to prime the next phase of the negotiation.

Priming in a Difficult Negotiation

Priming is an essential stage in a negotiation that centers around a complaint. You are a small-business owner who picks up the phone to hear Jake, an attorney client, who is upset and angry about an invoice. He has built up a head of steam, and feels indignant and wronged. His speech is rapid and pressured.

You have a choice. You can be defensive and refuse to talk to him until he is calmer, or you can listen. When you want to learn his concerns and negotiate a way to handle them, priming means creating an atmosphere for communication. Listen, don't interrupt, and wait until Jake has wound down. These are examples of soothing questions that pave the way for two-sided communication:

Tell me what's concerning you.

Let me hear your situation.

What were your expectations?

What would make you satisfied?

Understand how part of the limbic system works in our brains. The limbic system is set up to seek comfort. Jake is conveying to you that he is in a state of discomfort. When you use a soothing tone coupled with questions that show you really want to understand the person's perspective, you are conveying concern. You are trying to comfort and accommodate the person. You're setting the stage for saying, "Let's enter into this negotiation and I'm going to take care of you."

Suppose you reacted a different way. When Jake complained about the bill, you could have responded aggressively: "What are you talking about? You said you wanted us to bill you for 30 hours. We billed you for 25 hours. We gave you five extra hours for free. Are you mad? We don't need to be dealing with people like you. I'll tell you what; pay the invoice and we'll call this quits right here."

Suppose you adopted that particular stance. Most likely the lawyer would not have expected this kind of reaction. Depending on the personality type that other person has and to what degree you had leverage, the lawyer may acquiesce and say, "Wait a minute, I'm sorry. I really didn't understand all of the variables that went into this bill. Now that you say you gave us five free extra hours of nonbillable time, I'm very appreciative. We'll have the check in the mail to you tomorrow."

Your priming determines the next steps in the negotiation process. You also set the tone for how that negotiator will act with you in the future.

My motto is you're always negotiating. The reason I insist upon people understanding that is because that what you do today influences the next occurrence that you will engage in that could be a moment later with someone whom you're negotiating with. It also influences how the two of you will interact in the future. Be mindful of the fact that you are constantly priming the other individual as to how to interact and react to you. Consider if it would be strategic for you to use your leverage to be softer or harsher. You are in control. Remember, the action you engage in will have an affect the next time you negotiate with that negotiator.

Recognizing Priming

How do you recognize when people are using priming tactics against you? Just as you do research about your opponent, expect that others will do research about you. Don't be caught off guard. Be attuned to your reputation and what others say about your negotiation style. The other negotiator has an expectation as to how you're going to react in certain situations. Do you have a reputation as being easily angered? Are you known for your calmness?

Tom was known among his colleagues as a hothead. He flared into anger easily. His internist told him, "Tom, your blood pressure is too high. You need to learn some methods of controlling your anger. I would hate to see you have a stroke one day." With this in mind, Tom resolved to not allow himself get riled up when he got into negotiations.

The next day, one of Tom's coworkers, Victor, came storming into his cubicle. "What do you mean by this memo? Do you realize how bad it will make our department look?" Victor expected Tom to scream back. Tom leaned back in his chair to put distance between those words and how they affected him. After Victor finished his tirade, Tom leaned forward with a smile on his face and said, "Are you finished?" Tom threw him off by responding in a very calm manner. As he replied, "Let's talk about this when you are finished screaming," Tom watched Victor's reaction. Victor looked puzzled.

Victor started to wonder, "Wait a minute, I just had this guy back on his heels and he was literally leaning away from me so I knew my tactic was working—or was it?"

Tom took the priming aspect that Victor thought would be effective and turned it around against him to a point that Victor wondered: "What happened to the Tom I used to know? Does this guy know something that I don't necessarily know? Have I miscalculated the amount of leverage that I might have in this situation?" Tom's unexpected reaction put Victor into a quandary. Victor questioned his effectiveness in using such a priming technique against Tom.

I mentioned earlier in the chapter that you may prime your adversary in the middle of the negotiation based on what is occurring. For example, you are negotiating with Amy, who is an aggressive person. She shoves a document in your direction and says, "Look, this is the best deal you're going to get. Sign it or forget it!" Let's say you play along. You make your hands tremble. While sitting at a table next to her, you reach for the document and you look at it. To gain a height advantage over Amy, you stand up. After stopping your trembling, you say with confidence, "If this is the best deal that I'm going to get, I don't think we are going to have a deal." You rip the paper up into small pieces and allow each little sliver of paper to fall onto the table. Then you start to walk slowly out of the room.

At that point in time you will have turned Amy's tool of being antagonistic against her. Your knowledge of your leverage lets you see that you can still get a deal. Amy and you both know you have another choice; she knows her ploy of trying to prime you by displaying anger has truly backfired. Amy puts a hand on your shoulder and says, "Let's not be hasty. Let's sit down and talk."

I had a situation once when one of my clients had a lawyer. He had a nasty attitude when he called me. We were discussing what he called his "take it or leave it" position. I told him, "You can now tell your client that you were the one who blew this deal" and I hung up on him. He waited a few days and sure enough called back and tried to be nice. We ended up concluding the deal, but the point is, I let him know his tactic was not going to work. He assumed his priming aspect would be effective: He was rough and tough; after all he was a lawyer and I was "just" a business person. Remember the importance of learning about the other negotiator. Find out who you're dealing with.

Timing of Priming

You have a certain degree of control over when you use priming. For example, you can chose the time in a negotiation to display a different demeanor. As you analyze a situation, you may expect the other negotiator to respond in one particular manner. When it is to your advantage, you may apply a stimulus to get that negotiator to respond the way you wish. Consider your leverage points and who is not at the negotiation table. Ask yourself, "Where is this person getting her instructions? To what degree does she have the ability to go to a certain point in the negotiation and then stop because she's been told she could take this negotiation up to this line and no further?"

If that's the case and you have insight into how far she can go, you can push her to a point and understand that she can't go past this point. Now apply other stimuli to reveal her plan. She says, "I need to reconvene at another time," to which you say "Why?"

Her: "I need to assess what you have discussed thus far."

You: "What is it that you need to assess?"

Her: "I need to just think about this offer a little more."

You: "How might I be able to help you think about it a little more so as to help us move forward?"

What you're doing is making an assessment as to how much further she might be able to go. Your objective is to see to what degree she needs to go back and talk to somebody else. You are using that mind-set to not only cue her to change her perception of the negotiation, but you've also taken that time to gather more insight and information from her. This will arm you with more leverage that you can utilize later in the negotiation.

Priming at the end of the negotiation

You have reached the end of the negotiation and are ready to use priming to evaluate the firmness of the deal. Confirm your understanding of the covenants of the deal with the other individual by observing her body language at that time.

Is she smiling?

Is she receptive to the deal?

Test the vulnerability of certain aspects of the deal to see to what degree, based on her body language, that she might be amenable to meeting those obligations. I like to use this example: "You'll have a wire transfer to my bank for a million dollars by next Tuesday end of business day, correct?" You're smiling at your female opponent. You're literally leading her with your body language by nodding your head and saying "Yes." She says, "Yes, I definitely will," and she's nodding her head also. Contrast that to her not smiling or following your lead as you nod your head. If she starts to stammer, you know that she is somewhat hesitant as to whether she can deliver.

You might then say to her because you've sensed hesitancy, "I believe what you're saying. If the check is not there, just please understand I will have to accept this deal from another entity."

Now you've primed her to understand that if the wire transfer does not take place on Tuesday, the deal is off. Knowing how badly she needs the deal now, you have primed her to acknowledge she will lose the deal if the money is not there. That's one way that you can use priming to assure at the end of the deal that all the terms are actually met.

Here is another tactic you can use. Don't shake your opponent's hand at the end of the deal. Now remember that you've already primed her to know if she does not abide by the covenants of the agreement that the deal is off. You already know that she wants that deal and she wants it badly. It's commonplace for a handshake to occur at the conclusion of a deal. The failure to shake hands could signify that the negotiator is not enamored with this deal and has alternate plans.

Suppose you do not shake her hand at the conclusion of the deal. You say, "You'll have the money to us by next Tuesday, correct?" She says, "Yes, we will." Notice how she says this: Is her voice firm and assured? Does she display a level of commitment?

You respond, "Okay, I have to leave. I look forward to connecting with you after we receive that wire transfer next week. I'll talk with you then," and you're out the door. She's thinking to herself, "This guy is really serious." You are reinforcing from a priming perspective the fact that you have another deal in place if this one falls through. Her deal to you is not as important as she may have thought. You now have primed her to get this agreement completed. She's going to go ahead and make all the efforts that are needed. She may end up having that money to you by Monday just to show exactly how serious she is about abiding by the covenants of the deal because she needs it so badly.

This is another signal that you can perceive from her actions simply because you used a body language gesture of not shaking her hand to reinforce the position you placed her in from a priming position.

In Summary

Understand the effectiveness of priming. The environment can invoke pleasant memories associated with good times. By managing the environment, you can set the expectations for the interactions that are to occur as you actually enter into a negotiation.

Consider how the limbic system allows you to experience pleasure and avoid displeasure. When you experience displeasure you will seek comfort, and one way to lead someone into a more comfortable state is simply a smile. A baby's mother smiles and the baby starts to smile right back. The baby is experiencing comfort. The baby is hungry. The baby starts to cry to display his discomfort. That is not taught. That's innate. Those are factors that are innate in all of us. We all seek comfort when we are in a state of discomfort.

When it comes to priming, all you need to do is assess how you might be able to shift the perspective of your opponent from a state of comfort or discomfort. Apply the perfect stimuli in order to get the other negotiator to experience discomfort or comfort. You will be able to manipulate him by using stimuli throughout the negotiation.

It is important to efficiently plan how to use priming in a negotiation. Be adaptive in the negotiation; be aware of when you are experiencing comfort and discomfort. If you use a tactic that doesn't work and you thought it was going to produce a certain result, you're going to place yourself into a state of discomfort. Understand the impact that priming has in everyday aspects of our lives, especially in a negotiation because you're always negotiating.

Chapter 4

✸ ✸ ✸ ✸ ✸ ✸ ✸ ✸ ✸ ✸ ✸ ✸

Colors: *Controlling the Emotional Palette*

Adam, the Los Angeles–based man sitting next to me on the plane to Newark, New Jersey, was clearly nervous. He said, "As soon as we land, I am headed into an important meeting in Manhattan that will affect the future of my business. I am negotiating at a bank for a loan." In a glance, I spotted a problem. He wore a shirt with huge bright pink flowers and no suit jacket. "Adam, I suggest you make a stop at a menswear store before that meeting."

Colors can provide insight into a person's status. Consider this situation: I was the vice president of a company. I had on a freshly ironed white shirt, a red tie, and navy blue suit. The president was casually dressed in a yellow shirt and a pair of slacks. When the president and I walked into a seminar, a gentleman mistook me for the president. He said, "Sir, I would like to talk to you and your staff about how we can improve your business operations." The reason the gentleman approached me was because of the colors I was wearing and the fact that the president of the organization was dressed very casually. Colors project an image that will enhance or detract from your power as a negotiator.

The Meaning of the Power Suit

The power outfit I had on was a combination of navy blue, red, and white. Blue conveys stability, loyalty, wisdom, and intelligence. Red symbolizes energy. White is associated with purity. The combination projects someone who is energetic, truthful, and pure, someone who is good—just from the color combinations alone.

Usually people will have three colors on and sometimes two. They may have on a navy blue suit, a white shirt, and a red tie. They may have on a black suit, a yellow tie and a white shirt. That says something about that person's demeanor. The dark suit conveys formality and elegance. Look at the major color scheme that someone has on. When I say major, if the person had on a dark-colored suit, that would be the major component. Then look at the other combinations, the accessories that go along with the main color.

As you read this chapter, you will discover how colors and color combinations influence the perception people have of you.

Colors and Body Language

Your colors may provide clues about your personality. Outgoing people may wear more lively colors. Their colors may project the attitude of "I'm not afraid. I'm open. I want to be noticed.

Look at me!" People may wear drab colors if they don't want to attract a lot of attention.

Envision this: You're driving down the street and you see two pedestrians. One is dressed in dark colors and the other is wearing light-colored colors. More than likely you're going to notice the person in the lighter colors. Our eyes are drawn to light versus dark colors. This is why some people will choose to wear certain colors based on the influence that colors have on body language.

Consider another situation. A business owner is about to complete the last of several meetings to negotiate the sale of her business. She's wearing a well-tailored green jacket and black slacks. What is the significance of her clothing choice? Green is associated with money. The black slacks project elegance and formality. If you look at the combination of the colors she has on, she's projecting financial success, eloquence, and formality.

Shelley's eyes widened when she saw Woodrow enter the room. Woodrow was about 50 pounds overweight. He wore a bright yellow suit. Shelley thought, "What a clown!" She said, with a hint of sarcasm, "Nice suit, Woodrow." Missing the sarcasm, Woodrow said, "Thanks. I got it on the sales rack." Shelley thought, "I bet that suit was there for a long time before you bought it!"

Shelley made several assumptions about Woodrow when she saw him in the suit. First, she knew Woodrow lacked fashion sense. But second, she concluded he did not take himself or the situation seriously. The yellow suit made Woodrow look larger and less believable. Shelly found herself wanting the negotiation to be over quickly. She was afraid that she would laugh at his appearance if she stayed in the room with him. Whenever Shelley looked at Woodrow, all she could see was his suit.

Imagine Shelley's reaction if Woodrow came in wearing a black suit. The black suit would have not made him look more obese and would lend some elegance to his appearance. Coupled with a white shirt, the combination of black and white would express purity and make Woodrow more credible and appealing.

Color invokes a mind-set. Shelley would not take Woodrow seriously when he wore a yellow suit. Suppose Shelley leaned away from Woodrow while saying, "Yellow! You know most serious people don't wear yellow, especially yellow suits." Note that this aggressive statement would have told Woodrow that he was out of alignment with his environment. Shelley shifted some positional power in her direction. She enhanced her positional power through her body language; she acted repelled by his outfit. "I tell you what, Woodrow, let's reconvene tomorrow. I find myself unable to focus on our discussion. Your suit is blinding me."

Positional power is the power anyone will have throughout the course of a negotiation. It ebbs and flows from one negotiator to the other based on the offer that's been made, the value of the offer, and the intent of the positioning statements. Shelley used her positional power to control the negotiation and gain an advantage over Woodrow.

Let's look at this from a different perspective. Let's say Woodrow is a highly placed executive who had a momentary fashion lapse. He walked into the meeting wearing his yellow suit. There you are wearing your nicely tailored navy blue suit, white shirt, and red tie. You're ready for this negotiation. You are set. "Bring it on" is the mind-set that you have. In walks this guy with a yellow suit on. He has the power to give you what you need for your business. You stare at him and swallow the comment you were about to make. You defer to his positional power and focus your gaze on his face, avoiding looking at his yellow suit.

Colors and Culture

In today's world, you can be negotiating with a person from another country who comes from a radically different culture than yours. Consider the culture in which you are negotiating and adjust accordingly.

I wore a yellow velour shirt on my first day of junior high school. What a bad choice—one I remember years later! First of all, it was a hot day. Velour is a heavy material. Yellow really makes you stand out. I remember the older kids teased me by calling me a canary. They did so because in that culture it was not cool to stand out, especially by wearing yellow. Very few boys actually wore yellow.

In my desire to be accepted, I put myself outside of their boundaries and thus the same thing occurs when people are considering how they will negotiate in a particular culture. You can go anywhere in the world and find the two prominent colors that people use are black and white. If you are going to be negotiating based on someone's cultural background, understand if black has special meaning, such as evil. Knowing this will help you avoid wearing black. You might want to wear blue if that's more acceptable in that environment.

When I was in my mid-30s, my kids bought a shirt for me for Father's Day. The shirt had wide stripes of yellow, orange, green, and red. While wearing the shirt, I happened to walk by one guy and the guy said to me "Hey, that's really nice." I thought, "Okay." I was puzzled and kept walking. I happened to pass another guy and he said, "You know it's nice that you're not afraid to wear your colors." I thought, "What is he talking about? Not being afraid to wear my colors?" I finally understood based on the environment that I was in that these men assumed I was gay.

If I was negotiating in that culture and I had intentionally put that shirt on, I would have sent a message of, "I'm just like you." I would be creating an internal bonding process just by the colors that I had on. I would also be sending the signal that I was not afraid to be recognized for what I was if I were gay and had those colors on. That would influence the negotiation based on that culture.

I've described the impact of a man wearing a yellow suit and a woman wearing a green suit jacket with black slacks. Here are additional considerations for selecting your clothes. Know the environment in which you are negotiating and the message that you wish to send. As an example, I shared the strategy of entering a gay environment wearing clothes that would show alignment with the culture.

The same thing is true if you happen to be negotiating in an environment where you're an artist. You believe someone needs to perceive you as having the background that you possess in order to be more believable and more authentic.

Recall Adam, who was wearing a bright flowered shirt on his way to a business meeting to get a loan for his business. Adam did not follow my advice to stop at the menswear store. When he walked into the conference room, right away he saw a display of emotion on Ivan's face, who was a conservative banker. Adam read microexpressions that he interpreted as surprise and contempt, as well as dismissal. "You don't like my shirt?" he asked. Ivan dishonestly replied, "It is fine. Everything is good."

Suppose Ivan answered truthfully: "It's not what we normally see people wear when they're looking for such a substantial loan for their business." Now that Adam has drawn out the truth, he can explain, "As an artist I wear bright colors to express the creativity that I have."

Adam has worn the appropriate clothing for the discipline that he's involved in but the wrong clothes for the banker's world. He used his observation of microexpressions and body language to attempt to repair the damage. He scrambled to shift Ivan's mind-set and to establish positional power by helping Ivan see why Adam wore the flowered shirt.

You are standing in front of your closet the night before a critical negotiation, contemplating what you will wear the next day. Understand the environment in which you are going to be in and the impact of the colors you choose. To what degree are they aligned with the environment, the concepts of acceptable clothing choices, and the values of the other people present? Consider what you are trying to accomplish based on the mind-set of your opponent. You should be able to anticipate the impact colors have and the meaning that they have to that individual.

Consider the nature of the industry in which you are negotiating and the status of the other negotiator. How liberal or conservative is the industry? What do people usually wear who work within that industry? If you're going into a 9:00 to 5:00 banking environment, one that is conservative, you would not walk into that environment with a bright suit on because you would not be perceived as being serious. Knowing that, it would behoove you to go in wearing muted colors of navy, gray, or black. Be very aware of what environment you're going into. It is not helpful to your success as a negotiator to allow your clothes to act as an obstacle to achieving what you want during a negotiation.

Colors and Weight

When I was a kid, I went to the circus. I was always amazed at how the guy would accurately guess someone's weight before that person stood on a scale. One day I asked him, "How do you do it? What is the factor that helps you predict someone's weight?" "It's the colors they wear," he told me. "If people have on bright colors I will usually take away about five to 10 pounds, depending on my estimate of their size. If they have on dark colored clothes, I will usually add five or 10 pounds to my estimate."

I never forgot that simply because I realized he was adjusting his estimate based on colors; that's the influence that colors have on your appearance.

As any dieter knows, the colors you wear may make your body appear larger or smaller. You will notice when people want to look very elegant and slimmer they'll wear black. There are times when you want to appear smaller; you will wear darker colors to a negotiation. If you want to appear to be larger, you will wear lighter colors.

Once I was with a client who had on a blouse and suit jacket that were a little too tight for her body size. Her blouse was a very bright pink. She and I were talking about how we would be able to negotiate rates for bringing consultants into her business.

I kept noticing she was really uncomfortable. She repeatedly tried to pull her suit jacket over her blouse. She could not close her jacket. When I tried to narrow down the rate I would charge for my services, I watched her squirm. Initially I thought she was squirming because of the rate I proposed. I quickly came to understand through her body language that it wasn't the rate at all. I did that by testing a bracketed rate system. (A bracketed rate is the lowest rate I know I'd be able to accept to address her engagement and not lose money. In a negotiation you should always have a bracketed system in mind to indicate when you're at the high end of the bracket (i.e., the most you expected) and when you're at the low end (i.e., your walk-away point). The middle of that system is your sweet spot—one where you and the opposing negotiator should have the greatest possibility of being in agreement.)

What I realized was that it was the tightness of the clothes and the brightness of her blouse that was influencing her reactions. She was distracted by her clothing; that came through in her body language.

I've shared a little bit about clothing and picking out clothing while thinking ahead to the strategy you wish to project in a negotiation. Your body size and type should influence the clothes you're planning to wear.

Gauging Reactions to Colors

Keep in mind that some people are color blind and cannot recognize certain colors. But for the rest of the population, you can read body language to get insight into how someone perceives the colors you have on. Just watch microexpressions, such as eye movement, when you first enter into his environment.

- Does he give you a casual glance up and down?
- Do his eyes actually dilate?
- If so, what does that mean?

These microexpressions might mean the person likes the color combination that you have on. This gives you a clue as to how you might be able to negotiate with that person based on the colors that you have on.

Changing Your Colors during a Negotiation

Think about a negotiation you have been in when a person takes off a suit jacket. For example, Jeremy and Anita were attorneys who were negotiating to settle a personal injury suit. Jeremy was wearing a gray tailored jacket. As they hit an impasse in the negotiation, Jeremy took off his jacket to expose a white shirt. Anita watched the change in colors and pondered its meaning.

She considered the timing and reason for Jeremy removing his jacket. Why was he prompted to do so, and what was the message he was sending? For example, earlier in the chapter I shared that the white shirt displays innocence and purity. Anita wondered, "Is Jeremy trying to project an air of innocence? Is he sending a subliminal message of, 'I'm pure. I'm really open to the statement that you've just made'"?

Anita speculated, "Why did he take off his jacket at this point in the discussion? Is he really getting too hot also?" Anita thought, "This is a signal I should watch Jeremy more closely." She observed Jeremy to rub his eye, meaning, "I don't want to see this offer." Then he tugged at his collar. She wondered, "He could be saying, 'This is really making me hot under the collar.'" The removal of Jeremy's jacket caused Anita to watch his body language to add to her interpretation of why he took his jacket off and the meaning of the white shirt.

Consider the timing of the jacket's removal. Jeremy took it off when they hit an impasse. Was he saying, "Let me get down to work, roll up my sleeves, and dig into this negotiation so we can come up with a reasonable number"? Was he saying, "You can trust me. You see my white shirt, which is depicting purity and cleanliness. It's also depicting the fact that I can be trusted. There's safety in what I'm saying. You know you want to accept my offer, don't you"?

In addition to the thoughts Anita had about why Jeremy exposed his white shirt, she could have also considered if he was signaling surrender since he'd also tugged at his collar, and rubbed his eye. Take note of such signals when you're in a negotiation. If you're unsure as to a meaning at one point, pay attention to the signals that follow. The additional insight will help you validate what you'd sensed earlier.

You're in the middle of the negotiation and you have shifted your perspective. How do you use colors that you wear to reflect that change? One day you wear a conservative navy blue suit. At the end of the day you are not satisfied with the progress of the negotiation. The next day you wear a white suit. Your adversary asked you, "Are you okay?" "Why do you ask?" you respond. "Because you have on that white suit and it's not the norm." You reply, "Oh I'm feeling good. As a matter of fact, yesterday's negotiation went so well I thought I would just brighten things up."

Is that sarcasm? It is dependent upon how things went yesterday, but you've shaken up the dynamics. You have changed your outfit completely and gone in the opposite color direction from what you had on the previous day. You are sending a nonverbal signal of the fact that you have mentally changed: "Expect different techniques from me today."

Take into consideration all of these nuances to project body language signals during a negotiation.

Environmental Colors

As you have seen, colors influence the thoughts and strategies of negotiators. Note how you feel when you walk into a drab room. Bright colors stimulate you. Isabel was meeting with Homer to discuss providing a series of training sessions for his sales force. They were sitting in Homer's office, which had black walls. "Why am I having such trouble thinking of how to structure this deal?" Isabel wondered. "I'd hate to work in this office. It is like a cave!" Although Isabel was unaware the drab environment was stifling her creativity, she knew she wanted to escape the room. "Homer, do you think we could move to your conference room so I might be able to spread out my proposal?" Isabel felt an immediate lift in her mood when she moved into the brightly lit conference room.

Although black clothing may convey elegance, black can also symbolize death, evil, and mystery. Black walls can be depressing. When Isabel thought about that room, she wondered if Homer deliberately had negotiations in his office to control the tone of the discussion. The colors in the room may have a direct impact on the flow of the negotiation.

Testing Assumptions about Colors

You might for strategic reasons draw attention to the other negotiator's clothing by asking questions. It can be helpful to understand how the other person perceives colors based on his culture and body size. Let's say you are negotiating with Darin and have a two-day negotiation planned. Darin enters the room on the first of two days; he is wearing a yellow suit. You might assume Darin is wearing a yellow suit because he is oblivious to how heavy it makes him look. Test this by saying, "I've noticed that you're wearing a nice yellow suit today. Tell me, how do you feel when you wear it?"

Darin replies, "It makes me feel sharper." You ask, "What do you mean by sharper?" "It makes me think clearer. It makes me feel as though I have more energy," Darin clarifies.

Whatever Darin says enables you to decode his perspective of what he's wearing at that particular time. If, on the other hand, Darin says, "I like to wear yellow suits because I really don't really care what people think. I'm my own individual. I do what I want because I'm the one who blazes new trails for others to follow."

You're able to decode the fact that Darin does not care about how other people might judge him for wearing yellow. He likes the color and is going to wear it regardless of what others think. In deciding to test your assumptions about Darin, you go further: "Yellow is an unusual choice for businessmen who want to be perceived as serious." Darin gives you a blank stare.

Darin told you how he felt about his yellow suit on the first day of your two-day negotiation. On the second day, Darin came to the negotiation table wearing a different yellow suit. He heard what you said. You gave him your input. His nonverbal statement in this case said, "I told you before that I am of the mind-set that I'm a leader. I don't care what others think. Yellow is a color I like and I'm going to wear it." You've decoded the fact now and verified it not only through Darin's body language and nonverbal responses that he is someone who is different.

Having heard your message, suppose Darin came back the second day wearing a charcoal gray suit, yellow tie, and white shirt. Now you know you have altered his perspective; he has changed his mind-set about the appropriateness of what he should wear. You've also tested his assumptions about his freedom as a leader to wear whatever he wanted. Now his nonverbal message is, "I heard what you said. I rethought it. I realize I could have more impact if I fall in line with your expectations. I am willing to change."

Darin's willingness to change shows how open he is to change; this has implications for your strategies during the negotiation. You've learned that when challenged, Darin backs down. You take note of Darin's changes based on the colors that he was wearing and that he wore a darker-colored suit on the second day. You know that you've truly influenced him and caused him to alter his perspective.

Lest I mislead you, remember that you could make all kinds of assumptions about color that could be wrong. Keep in mind that unusual color choices or clothing may not be deliberately made. You might be putting too much stock into your interpretation of a color combination when literally the person stood in front of his closet and grabbed the first thing that was at hand before coming to that negotiation. I have seen people in color combinations or clothing that were unusual at best. I stood behind a woman in a line at an airport gate who had put on her shirt backwards. It had a little pocket that was over her back instead of in the front.

Even if someone has on a black suit with a white shirt and a yellow tie, it's a different mind-set than the person who has on a yellow suit with a white shirt and a black tie. Yellow has become the predominant color with that suit being a larger piece of clothing.

Let's say the person has on orange, black, green, and purple. You think to yourself that the person is color blind. You might also speculate that the person doesn't care how he looks and if you make that assumption, you then carry that over to what else might he not really care about. There is a danger in making assumptions based not only on the color combinations that people wear but how they look in those color combinations. Some people look better even if they have on the same color combinations if they're wearing vertical versus horizontal stripes. When that's the case you have to give thought to what was he thinking in wearing that garment. Exotic color combinations can be very distracting when you're actually in a negotiation.

Decoding the Meaning of Colors

As I have mentioned up to this point, several factors influence the meaning of color, including culture, occupation, and status. Here are some generalizations about colors.

Red

Red is associated with energy, but it's also paired with war, danger, strength, power, determination, passion, desire, and love. You may have heard of prostitution in a "red-light district."

Most people first think of power when they consider the color red. Earlier in this chapter I mentioned the red tie as part of a power suit. You've heard of the power suit or the power outfit, and it usually has red associated with it. Red is a dominating color. Men are definitely drawn from a psychological perspective toward red more so than women. It's part of the makeup of men.

A group of researchers experimented with the impact of red in drawing attention to an object. They put a dollar bill on the ground and watched as people walked by to see who would pick the dollar bill up. Nine out of 10 people who walked past the dollar bill picked it up. The researchers changed the conditions by putting a red line down on the ground, and then placed the dollar bill right beside the red line. The exact opposite happened. Ten people would go by the dollar bill; one would pick it up and the other nine would bypass it.

When the people who bypassed it were asked why, initially some said, "I don't know. There was something that wasn't right with bending over and picking up that dollar bill." After the researchers suggested that maybe the red line had something to do with it, the research subjects said, "You know, now that you're saying that, I guess I was sensing danger. It's a trick, something was not right." Red has that ability to influence people.

Orange

Orange originates from red and yellow. In so doing, the color of orange actually takes on some of the properties of red's energy aspect and it takes on the property of the joy of yellow. It also has the connotation of the tropics. Orange is associated with gaiety, happiness, and the fun environment of tropical surroundings. Orange has the power to put you into a mood, a mind-set, whereby you feel a little happier than you normally would. You will wear such colors in the summertime, you'll notice. Orange is associated with nice weather. You don't see people walking around a lot in the winter with orange on, although they may wear orange during the autumn harvest season.

Yellow

Sunshine yellow invokes not only joy and happiness, but it also represents intellect and energy. We all know how much energy comes from the sun. Yellow injects that perspective into your mind-set. People in an environment with a lot of yellow tend to get more excited. You might not want to put somebody with whom you are negotiating in a yellow room if you want to avoid excitement.

Green

Green is paired with money, nature, fertility, growth, and harmony. Green is associated with freshness. It's vibrant, healthy, and good for you. You may have heard of the green grocer who sells fresh food.

Blue

Blue is associated with stability, trust, and loyalty. I have mentioned blue throughout this chapter. Blue has the connotation of someone who is wise, confident, smart, honest, and faithful. "I'll be true blue to her." You may have heard that expression in the past; blue conveys such sentiments because of its attributes.

Purple

I love purple. Not only from a branding perspective does it convey energy, but it also has the components of blue from which energy stems, which is also found in the colors of red and orange.

Along with that energy aspect, purple symbolizes power, nobility, luxury, and ambition. It is associated with royalty.

When I considered making purple part of my brand it was because I liked the color without fully understanding about the characteristics associated with it and its impact on others. The more I learned what certain colors meant, I understood why it had that effect on me. I am ambitious and I like nice things in life. People have told me that I'm powerful in certain situations. The color happens to denote exactly those characteristics about me.

Consider how people can incorporate a color into clothing. When I negotiate, I often wear a dark-colored suit, a white shirt, and always a purple tie. Think about what that is saying from a color combination perspective. The dark-colored suit is emanating power and elegance while the purple tie is radiating energy, power, and nobility. I'll usually have on a white shirt and a white handkerchief in my jacket pocket, or one that is a combination of purple or white. I send out that cohesive signal of radiating power, nobility, purity, and energy in so doing.

White

White is associated with goodness, innocence, and purity. It also symbolizes safety along with cleanliness, and it has the added value of depicting faith. A bride wears white on her wedding day to symbolize the purity that she possesses. In most societies, white is good and black is not so good. The guy with the white hat in the United States is always depicted as the hero. The guy in the black hat is always the villain.

Black

Black indicates power, elegance, and formality. It also indicates death, evil, and mystery. We associate black with death and mourning. People wear black to a funeral to convey grief. Men have to be very cautious about wearing an all-black outfit. A black suit and black shirt has a criminal connotation. All black has more of an indication of death, evil, and mystery than if you lightened it up by wearing some of the other accessory colors. The body language signal that you're actually sending if you had on all black would be one of "Caution! Don't get too close to me. You don't know what I might be up to." That's the mystery aspect. Conversely, a woman who dresses in all black might be viewed as sophisticated.

You'll also notice when police officers or the National Guard are in a situation where they have to put down a riot they will have on all-black garb because that's intimidating. Can you imagine if they had on all pink or all yellow? That might be another way to put down a riot because people would be laughing so much that they wouldn't be able to do anything else. Therein lies the different color schemes and the influence that such can actually have in a negotiation or any other environment in which you find yourself in.

Combatting Distracting Colors

Earlier, I shared two examples of how to avoid being manipulated by distracting colors: You decided to look at your opponent instead of at his yellow suit. Isabel asked Homer if they could move to a brightly lit conference room to get out of a black-walled office. These negotiators were aware of the impact of the colors in the environment.

This chapter is designed to help you understand what colors typically mean. But you can deliberately tune out the connotations of colors and assign your own meaning. Suppose you said to yourself, "Wait a minute. Look at these guys in their suits and ties. I'm going to be as strident as I wish to be and go against the grain by wearing my bright suit. I'm not going to be manipulated by them at all." You have to be aware of the risks associated with the degree you put yourself outside of the normal boundaries with such a mind-set. Nevertheless, you can do so to keep yourself from being manipulated by colors or people's associations with colors.

There's a politician that was a TV reality person at one time. He used his positional power to have his minions actually tell people how to interact with him, sometimes to the degree of what colors to wear before they met him. As an example, they told people, "Don't shake his hand. He doesn't like shaking hands with people." The first thing the politician would do as soon as that person came into his environment was shake his hand. Right away that person would think, "Wait a minute, I was told he doesn't like to shake hands." The politician used this strategy to manipulate others.

If you are aware that certain color schemes occur in an environment, you can choose not to be manipulated by it. For example, Isabel could have said to herself, "I find Homer's office dark. I will view it as restful instead of depressing."

In Summary

Always consider the negotiation environment that you are going to be in and how different color schemes are perceived. Think through why you should wear a certain color scheme in a particular environment. I hope I have emphasized why you should never randomly select clothes from your closet before an important negotiation.

Do you wish to send the signal of being self-reliant and not necessarily one that follows the lead of others? If so, you may think about wearing the exact opposite colors that would be the norm for such an environment.

The colors of clothing and a room send messages that influence a negotiation. Harness this knowledge to control your appearance and observe the other negotiator's clothing. By being aware of the role of colors, you can deliberately send messages to others, as well as recognize the messages others are sending to you.

Be aware of the signals colors actually send and how they influence you from a body language perspective. Your effectiveness as a negotiator is based in part on the image you project and how you wear your power. The better you feel based on the colors that you have on, the more likely you will complete a successful negotiation.

Chapter 5

✦ ✦ ✦ ✦ ✦ ✦ ✦ ✦ ✦ ✦ ✦ ✦ ✦

Brain Games: *Understanding the Role of Emotions and Psychology in Negotiation*

Juan Martinez was in trouble. The rent was due on the gas station he leased. The falling price of gas was affecting his business. He operated his business with a very small profit margin; he was horrified to watch his profits steadily decline. Juan's wife was pressuring him to buy a house in a safer but more expensive location. With no savings, Juan felt trapped between his landlord and his wife. He felt like a failure—less of a man—when his wife said, "If you can't make more money from this business, maybe I will have to go to work."

When Enrique, Juan's landlord, called about the late rent payment, Juan felt the fear pervading his voice. "We have got to talk," he told his landlord. Enrique smiled as he heard the fear in Juan's voice. He thought, "How can I use this to my advantage?"

The combination of pressure from Juan's wife and landlord made Juan think, "Now something else to deal with!" Juan was stressed by the conversation with his wife. Trying to negotiate under stress means you are at risk for missing nonverbal signals. What Juan should have done was instead say to Enrique, "I'd like to call you back a little bit later," giving himself some time to reflect upon the situation as opposed to communicating in a state of fear.

Instead, Enrique concluded, "I'm in the driver's seat," and rightfully so. Enrique sensed that Juan was fearful and therefore more apt to do things more harmful to his negotiation position. Enrique figured, "I have more leverage." He knew he could probably push a little harder if he chose to do so, using Juan's fears to get him to capitulate.

Psychological Blocks

Fear is one of the strongest psychological blocks. *Anger* can function in the same way to block a negotiation. You've heard the expression, "I saw red." This implies the person lost the ability to accurately perceive the stimuli with a narrowed field of vision. *Disgust* also acts as a block, as I shared in Chapter 2 on microexpressions.

Surprise happens to be a psychological block or enhancement that influences our ability to negotiate because a lot of people do not like surprises. When we're surprised we have to go through the assessment as to whether or not a surprise is beneficial to us. Once we determine if the surprise is beneficial or detrimental to us, then we adopt a course of action. Surprise disables our ability to effectively negotiate.

These blocks influence your ability to negotiate. You will look at the other negotiator in a different light as a result of being fearful of what she may actually do to you. If you are angered by her actions, you may react in kind. Her intent may have been something completely different but because of the way you reacted you're putting her into the same type of state that you are in. Then the negotiation starts to go astray. Be cognizant of your mental attitude and how that causes you to be influenced by mental blocks when you're negotiating.

A Closer Look at Emotions

I have seen speakers placing a lot of importance on getting a speaking engagement. It is easy to fall into a trap of feeling desperate to book an engagement: "What do I need to do to get this gig? I'll discount my fee, not insist on 50 percent of my fee up front, pay my own travel expenses . . . ." and they end up giving away too much. They have a psychological block fueled by fear.

Be aware of what you fear, why you fear it, and to what degree your assessment of it is accurate. Consider how you reacted in other situations in the past when you felt fearful during a negotiation. Is the current situation identical to the one in the past? How did you handle the prior negotiation? What did you learn from the situation? How can you apply that information? Once you make those assessments, at least you know why fear is there and how to deal with it.

Contempt for your opponent may act as a psychological block. Even before you enter into a negotiation you think to yourself, "I'm going to pull this person down a peg or two. He got the better of me in the last negotiation. Now it's time for me to get even with him or at least let him know I'm not the chump he thought I was." Contempt means you'll react differently than if you had no psychological blocks to influence your negotiation style.

Sadness influences your ability to negotiate. You may feel besieged, depressed, or unhappy like Juan did as a result of talking to his wife before speaking to Enrique. Sadness puts you at a disadvantage because of what you're focused on—your emotion rather than the negotiation.

Benefits of Addressing Blocks

Understand the source of blocks and how you need to address them before you enter into the negotiation and the benefits you can get from doing so. If you focus on the outcomes both you and the other negotiator are striving to achieve, you will influence your frame of mind. Determine what you might have to address in order to give the other negotiator what she needs to make her feel fulfilled and thus give you what you need from the negotiation. Psychological blocks may cause a quick deterioration in a negotiation.

Liam Donnelly entered a car dealership to buy a car for his mother. Despite his best efforts negotiating with Morris Bass, the salesman, he got nowhere. After he left the car dealership, he got a call from Morris the next day: "Please come back in." Liam concluded they had gotten over that hurdle from the previous day and the discussion would go more smoothly when he returned to the dealership. That was Liam's perspective; think of Liam's frame of reference before he walked into the dealership.

To Liam's surprise, when he got to the dealership he found Morris wanted to start the negotiation again from the beginning. Liam said, "No, that's not where we were. I thought we had a deal, which is why I came back." The mind-set Liam had and the discovery that he was being thwarted caused him to blow up. He screamed about the practices the dealership used and that he would never purchase a car from them. All activity in the dealership stopped as people listened to Liam's voice. Liam's loss of control stemmed from his block. Had he thought through the whole situation, he would have realized the origin of his block. If Liam could have controlled his emotions, he might have been able to negotiate a deal.

Self-Esteem and Ego as Blocks

We all have a picture of who we are. While we assume others see us in a certain way consistent with our own beliefs, that is not always the case. For example, the opponent may be a suspicious person who believes that all people lie in an effort to manipulate a deal. It is much more difficult to negotiate with such a person. After all, he does not share the value that I have of myself as an honest person. Look at this from a different angle. Suppose you don't have the perspective your opponent is worthy of negotiating with you, meaning the person's position is too low within the organization. You're not going to negotiate with this individual in the same light as you would somebody else.

Let's also take into consideration the fact that you think this person is out to get you. When you start a negotiation with that mind-set, it will influence the way you will interact with the person. You will not tend to be as open as you otherwise might be because you may believe you'll be taken advantage of if you are open with your opponent. It is not surprising you will be leery or skeptical of offers that he might put on the table. Driven by self-protection, you will scrutinize offers for potential dangers and traps. You don't trust the opponent. Trust is essential in a negotiation.

Awareness of Psychological State

When we are in a stressful situation or a stressful environment, we just don't function as well as we otherwise could; we won't look at things from the same perspective. We may overlook something that could prove to be beneficial to us simply because we are distracted by fear and doubt.

At the same time, we get pulled deeper into a negotiation process, to our detriment. In a dogged way, we continue a negotiation without the full ability to concentrate. Our preoccupation with fear may lead us to see dangers where none exist, to be suspicious, and to overreact. We focus on the negative instead of the positive.

If you're not in the proper mind to negotiate, first of all, realize that's not the time for you to negotiate. The pitfall of negotiating in that type of mind-set is you may be more likely to make concessions; you may say something or do something that you otherwise would not have done had you been in a different frame of mind.

What you do today influences tomorrow's outcomes. You may be setting the seeds for future negativity when and if you ever negotiate with that individual or his associates. He might have said something negative about you, the way you negotiate, your personality, and so on.

For example, talking about the right mind-set, I had an inquiry from an organization to address a possible speaking engagement. I knew the person with whom I was talking had only one function: to gather information about the cost. I asked her questions such as, "Tell me exactly what it is that you're seeking as the result of bringing somebody in to speak." She clarified, "We want somebody to talk about body language." I asked, "What outcome are you really seeking?" "So the people will know how to read body language better," she replied. I responded, "In particular, what would you like them to know?" She admitted, "I'm not exactly sure." I probed, "How long would you want the presentation to last?" She said, "I'm not sure."

I inquired, "Can you please tell me your function in the organization and exactly how you came by my information?" "I did a search, found your information as a body language expert, and reached out to you," she said. Still looking for more information, I responded, "What else are you seeking from the whole engagement?" She acknowledged, "I'm not really sure. I need to know how much you cost."

A bit offended, I corrected her: "First of all, it's not a cost. It's an investment." I asked her how many people would be in attendance, and she said 200 to 300 people who would be Realtors. I summarized, "Okay, 200 to 300 people. It's not a cost, it's an investment because to the degree they become a lot better at deciphering body language they can negotiate better. Speaking of which, to what degree would you want the presentation to encompass negotiation tactics or strategies?" Her response was, "I don't know. I just need to know how much you cost." Feeling a bit like I was spinning in a circle, I said, "As I said, it's an investment."

When I momentarily took a step back, I realized with whom I was dealing. I asked her the question that we all need to know when we're negotiating: "Who else is involved in the decision-making process? Who will end up making the final decision?" She told me the CEO and the accounting VP.

She reemphasized she was just collecting data. "I can't really quote an investment figure," I told her, deliberately using the term *investment figure* because I did not want to be seen as a commodity. I'm not a commodity. I did that to differentiate myself. In a negotiation you always want to differentiate how what you're offering is different from someone else. In so doing you disqualify others with the same type of services.

Her final statement was, "I don't understand anything you said so I'm not going to go further." I said, "Okay, fine. Thank you." I then called the CEO of the organization. I left a voicemail message describing my credentials and if he wanted to reach out to me he could do so.

After reflection about my demeanor, I called the assistant back the next day and said I wanted to apologize. "I place a high emphasis on always communicating efficiently with people. It is my intention to get along with as many people as I possibly can. That did not occur yesterday and I called just to apologize." She said, "Thank you so much, Greg. You don't have to apologize, because I was just trying to collect information and they really did not give me a lot to go on." As we talked, I got additional information (that I already knew), but I made an ally inside of that organization whereby hopefully she will say, "I did reach him and by the way here's the information I gained from him."

Let's think about how I used leverage in that case. I mentioned to her that I called the CEO. I said, "I called him because I know the training that I provide is not only of benefit, but I've gotten feedback to indicate that from Realtors." Next, I asked her if she knew certain prominent individuals in the real estate field. When she admitted she did not, I knew her lack of knowledge about the industry confirmed she was just gathering information. In so doing I also gave her some insight as to how she could be better prepared if she did decide to gather more information.

Even though I was helping her, my assistance could be detrimental because I gave her names of people she might contact. But at least she knows that I was there to support her too. I closed that whole loop on being mindful of my demeanor and altering her perception of me and what initially took place.

The Medium for Negotiating

Consider how much information is conveyed through body language and voice. If I said to you "I love you," you would listen to the tone of my voice. If I wrote the words, "I love you," you get a feeling of what those words mean, but those words may have a different interpretation to you than they do to me. They may not convey the same intensity. You can gain more insight when you can hear the opponent's voice. Speaking to a person sitting in the same room with you yields more information than if you talk on the phone. Negotiating via e-mail or letters provides even less useful data.

The medium in which you negotiate gives great impact to how your message will be perceived, but at times you want to use different mediums. Adroitly use the medium to enhance your negotiation strategies. For example, it may be quite useful to make a written offer to ensure your opponent understands the terms of the agreement. This negotiation sets a different tone than if the agreement was verbal. You might make a tentative offer in writing and someone says, "Wait a minute, that's not what I understood we agreed to." Now you are able to point to a document that defines the scope of the agreement.

A written agreement gives you another perspective when you're talking to your opponents on the phone or in person. If they respond by preparing a letter that states, "That's not what I understood," you can clarify the details in writing, over the phone, or in person. Be mindful of what medium you use to communicate when you're negotiating. If you want to pick up the nonverbal signals, do so by communicating via phone or in person.

Body language enables you to pick up the nuances that people use to convey their emotions based on their pace, words, and excitement—you won't pick that up in writing. Understand what serves you best depending on what environment you're in and what you're trying to achieve with your communications.

For example, Attorney Kirk Wood called an engineering expert, Lorraine Nutting, and requested a report to be completed within eight days. Lorraine had worked for other attorneys in his firm, but she had never talked to him before. Kirk discussed the project, what was involved, and what he wanted. Lorraine took notes during the conversation, completed the project within eight days, and sent her invoice for the hours that exceeded the initial retainer. According to Lorraine's fee agreement, the timing of the report production qualified as a rush job.

Kirk disputed the invoice because he claimed he did not request the work to be done in a rush. Lorraine pointed out that he signed a fee agreement that specified the job would be a rush and he paid a rush rate retainer. When Lorraine supplied a photocopy of her notes, which gave the due date eight days after the phone call, Kirk stopped disputing the rush rate request.

Kirk also claimed he asked Lorraine to limit the project and not do such a complete report. Lorraine had nothing in writing from the attorney and no notes that confirmed the attorney's recollection. She had no recall of him making this request. There is a Chinese proverb: "The palest ink is better than the best memory." In this case, a letter that confirmed Kirk's expectations would have aided the collections negotiations. Had Lorraine and Kirk been negotiating via the medium of writing, they would have had a record of what Kirk wanted. It would have been difficult for him to wiggle out of that situation based on what he had written.

People honestly forget things sometimes. They have their own perspective and sometimes they'll blend two different thoughts together that came from two different sources. The more they think about that situation, the more they rely on their idea of reality and thus they're not lying. Their perspective is that this is exactly what happened. That becomes extremely difficult to deal with because the opponent has a different perspective of what was said, heard, and requested.

Lorraine gave Kirk exactly what she thought he wanted and needed. By not putting it in writing, both Lorraine and Kirk mistakenly believed they were in agreement about what Kirk wanted. In reality, nothing could have been further from the truth.

Suppose the same confusion occurred between friends. The strength of the relationship would encourage each to find a resolution. The friends value keeping their relationship intact. Kirk and Lorraine had no real intrinsic motivation to keep their relationship intact. Lorraine was at more of a disadvantage than Kirk was because her collection options were limited. She had already turned over her report. She could lower the price; she could ask him to pay what he thought was fair. She could write off her invoice and say she'd never do business with Kirk or his firm again. The point is Lorraine's work would not be compensated at the rate that she should have received simply because she did not have the agreement in writing. Kirk ultimately paid Lorraine about two-thirds of what he owed her.

Avoiding Disputes Based on Memory

Here's the step that should have occurred between Kirk and Lorraine; it's a good lesson for anyone who is engaged in a negotiation. One of the things that you should always do is to make sure both parties are in agreement about the covenants of the negotiation. Lorraine might have given Kirk her notes before she started work, saying, "This is my understanding. Please confirm it's yours." Having Kirk's endorsement of the plan would have averted the situation Lorraine faced.

Lorraine did not expect to encounter a collection issue with Kirk. Just because she had successfully dealt with other attorneys from the firm did not mean that Kirk would be like them. Be very mindful of your mind-set when you enter into a negotiation. Had Lorraine thought, "I've worked for this firm but not this attorney," she would have recognized she was negotiating with different people. You can do the exact things you did with person number one, and you will get a different outcome when you repeat those strategies with person two. Every negotiation is different. This is true even if you're negotiating with the same person based on that person's psychological outlook and mental blocks about what occurred in between the negotiations.

Subliminal Messages

We send subliminal messages to people all day long. They are projected in the way we walk and dress, the possessions that we have, and the cars we drive. You can send a subliminal message to the other negotiator by the way you simply walk into the room. Do you project confidence or intimidation? What messages do you send when you gesture? Do you move your hands in a random way, or do you drive points home with a pointed finger or a closed fist? All of those variables send subliminal messages.

Effective use of subliminal messages enhances your negotiation. Recall Liam Donnelly's reaction at the car dealership. One of the things he realized he could have done in addition to altering his demeanor was to set up Morris with subliminal messages. Liam could have said, "When I come back in we are going to reach a satisfactory deal. These will be the terms of the deal."

The subliminal message was, "We're going to reach a satisfactory deal." Liam might have tested that premise. Had Liam used a subliminal messaging technique of letting Morris know they would have a successful deal, he could have elicited

Morris' perspective. Responding to the trigger words, "successful deal," Morris would define the parameters of the agreement he would offer.

A negotiator might take a hard stance by saying, "If we can't reach a deal in this manner, there's no need for us to negotiate." Instead, lead the negotiation by saying, "I know we can reach a successful agreement." Then you state what a successful agreement means to you. Follow your description with a question: "Would you agree to that?" The opponent's response gives you an opportunity to ask follow-up questions. This technique allows you to present a subliminal message without coming right out and saying, "This is what I need to do."

Let's talk about subliminal messaging in a different perspective. Subliminal messages may be used to set expectations from a positive perspective, but also from a negative perspective. Suppose you're negotiating with someone who really needs the deal. You say, "If this deal doesn't come together, I know there's going to be a huge price to pay." The subliminal message is if you don't get this deal you're the one who is going to be suffering. That's a subliminal message, but you don't want to necessarily push your opponent into a corner by letting her know that you recognize she needs the deal much more than do you.

This type of subliminal message allows your opponent to save face. Never put someone in a negotiation position whereby she can't save face because she will use strategies, even in an unreasonable way, to maintain her reputation.

Emotional Intelligence

Emotional intelligence means being acutely aware of how you react in certain situations, which triggers will elicit certain reactions both in you and your opponent. It can also encompass the mannerisms you display in a particular negotiation environment given the position you are trying to convey. Do you want to be perceived as being someone who's easygoing versus hard-nosed?

When it comes to emotional intelligence, understand the role you wish to adopt and anticipate the one the other negotiator will adopt. Consider how you're going to interact with the other negotiator so you can effectively use triggers to produce the results you are seeking. When you are effective in controlling your and your opponent's emotions, you will become a more successful negotiator.

Fear's Effects on Emotional Intelligence

I started this chapter describing Juan and his conversation with Enrique and the fear that Juan was experiencing due to his wife and landlord pressuring him. Fear hampers emotional intelligence because it hinders our ability to think properly. We lose our ability to rationally evaluate the realities we are facing. Fear increases stress and impairs your performance.

It may be to your advantage to invoke fear in your opponent. This technique adds to your strategies for manipulating the other negotiator into a position whereby he sees the value in making the concession that you are requesting. For example, you may discuss what he would lose if he did not agree to the deal. Fear of loss motivates him to do what you say he should do because you have conveyed to him it's in his best interest.

When it comes to fear and emotional intelligence, be very mindful of how fear can influence your ability not only from an emotional intelligence perspective of negotiating efficiently, but at the same time how you can use fear on the other negotiator. Use fear to help him in performing to his best.

Juan was able to sense fear in his body as soon as he heard Enrique's voice. With that awareness, rather than reveal his fear, Juan could have postponed the call instead of the way that he handled the situation. "Why am I feeling so fearful? What can I do to reduce my stress?" Juan might have asked. Stress can destroy a negotiation. It makes you less aware of nuances, of options, and of strategies you may use. Stress robbed Juan of his ability to effectively negotiate. Juan needed a time-out to regain his composure. Had Juan halted the conversation, he would have gained time to reflect on Enrique's demeanor and what Juan needed to do to mollify him. "Yes, the rent is late. What might I be able to offer you in order to pacify you?"

Here's something else that Juan could have done. He could have recognized that he was feeling the effects of the pressure from his wife and the landlord. It's easier said than done to realize, "I'm carrying the weight of a prior situation into this one." The more the simultaneous stresses build up and you try to carry those into another negotiation the less likely you are to negotiate efficiently. Inevitably, you are at risk for making concessions.

Look at negotiations from the positive perspective to the degree that you can. Learn from the outcome of them as opposed to berating yourself: "I was so stupid." Instead, look at the positive aspects of your experiences. From an emotional intelligence perspective you will have buttressed up your fortification for future negotiations.

There's no such thing as failure. There are just unexpected outcomes. I often say I never fail. "What do you mean?" I am asked. I say, "I never fail no matter what the outcome is because I extract the good that lies within the situation and take it as a learning experience to improve my future negotiations." Staying positive aids your negotiation abilities. Complaining and negative behavior hampers performance and attracts more negativity.

Success Factors

Get the proper amount of rest before a negotiation. When you are tired you're likely to make mistakes that you otherwise would not make.

Part of being able to negotiate at top levels is to eat well. Foods and beverages give you a level of energy. High levels of caffeine may make you jittery. Eating too much before a negotiation may make you feel sluggish and less agile when you need to be in a negotiation.

Psychological Success Factors

Consider how to use your emotional intelligence to recognize which triggers to use with your opponent. Anticipate which ones will be employed against you to activate hot buttons as I describe in the next chapter. Hot buttons cause you to react to certain messages or situations.

What might occur as you go throughout the negotiation process? In your planning stage, prepare for every scenario that you are able to anticipate; envision the difficult aspects of the negotiation. Ask someone to prepare you through role play. Have the person assume the role of the other negotiator and the negative situation you might find yourself in. Work out your strategy, then switch roles. You become the negative person who you might negotiate with; you see other aspects of how you might be able to maneuver *before* you actually negotiate with that person.

By doing the role play scenario I described, you will also be better prepared to take one action versus another if you find yourself in that situation. You have already gone through it in your mind's eye. Psychologically, you're prepared for it; you are not caught off guard. You have procedures that you've thought about to put in place using principles of psychology to become a much better negotiator.

Subliminal Messages at an Impasse

Earlier I described how to use subliminal messages to make subtle suggestions such as, "When we complete this successful negotiation we'll both be happy with the outcome." Subliminal messages are also effective when you reach an impasse. You've hit a wall or so you think. What I mean is just because you reach an impasse today does not mean you cannot get passed it tomorrow. As long as you keep the door open you can continue the negotiation. You never want to slam it shut or back that person into a corner by saying, "Take it or leave it!"

Instead, use a subliminal message such as, "It seems like right now we're not going to be able to come to a suitable understanding. How about if we pick up this tomorrow, next week, or whatever timeframe and see if we can reach an admirable outcome at that time?" The subliminal messaging words "right now" implies that's only for the moment and it doesn't have to be that way forever.

So far I identified how to use subliminal messages with the other negotiator. As you become more attuned to subliminal messages, you may detect when the other negotiator is using them against you. As you're going through the planning stage you try to think of everything that might occur in the negotiation. Part of that process also is to consider what type of subliminal messages the other negotiators might use on you. What type of information do they have about you to frame their own subliminal messages? What are your own hot buttons and how might the opponent hit them with subliminal messages?

For example, when I was a kid other kids made disparaging comments about their adversaries' mothers. Kids sent subliminal messages just to start a fight at times with a child who was not smart enough to understand what was being done to him. Had the child been smart enough to understand the subliminal message that was being used, he could have denied the insult was not true and walked away from the situation. That's one way you can combat subliminal messages being used against you.

Understand what and how subliminal messages are used. Prepare for them; be careful about being swayed by them. If it is not to your advantage, don't give the response the other negotiator is seeking from you. Observe what he does based on your response. If he realizes subliminal messages aren't working on you, he will then more than likely try a different subliminal message. Watch for that tactic and observe what he does if you don't react the way he expects you to. This technique allows you to combat his subliminal messages.

You might be caught off guard as the result of your opponent using the subliminal message against you. Be as prepared as possible by getting the proper amount of rest, nutrients, and exercise.

I recall hearing the story of an elderly woman who was a plaintiff in a personal injury case. The attorney taking her deposition gave her pastries before the event started. He moved closer to her as he asked her questions, and did everything he could to ingratiate himself. Finally, as he nodded his head "yes" at her, he asked, "You don't really remember what happened in this accident, do you?" Imitating his body language, she nodded "yes." She was thoroughly convinced he was charming, and oblivious to the fact that her testimony had just ruined her case. At the end of the deposition, she turned to the attorney representing her and asked, "Why can't you be as nice as him?" After that experience, her attorney warned all of his clients about the subliminal messages they would encounter in the deposition room.

When you are a prepared negotiator, you will recognize the opponent is trying to push your buttons. You will have the insight to be able to think, "I can't do this. I have to be mindful of his strategies." For example, your adversary says, "I know you want to conclude this deal today; that is important to you." You might respond, "Oh no, I have all the time I need to reach a successful conclusion; I am in no hurry." Catch your opponent off guard by responding in the opposite manner than he expects.

Psychology of Bundling

Take advantage of the psychology of bundling to reach an agreement. Here's how this works. You have an offer the other negotiator likes, but he doesn't like it well enough to enter into a final agreement with you. Instead, he says something like, "If you add these elements I can seal the deal." You think, "No, that will make the deal unattractive to me. But I could offer him something else I'm prepared to surrender."

Understanding Your Motivation

You may have heard the expression, "To thine own self be true." Understand yourself and your values. Know why you do what you do and what influence others have on you. Consider how you influence others.

- What is it you want from others?
- Why do you connect with certain people versus others?
- What is it you are seeking as a result of doing so?

The more you understand how you are motivated and demotivated the more effectively you can interact. In any negotiation the first thought that any negotiator should have is, "How am I going to control myself in this negotiation?"

In Summary

Be mindful that brain games occur. Don't get upset when your opponents try to put you into a position that is advantageous to them. After all, you're negotiating. Everyone goes into a negotiation with the belief they will improve their position. Understand your opponent is trying to do the exact thing that you are trying to do.

Look for common ground to build trust. Think about what will occur if trust is broken and be prepared to deal with that too. Do you apologize to show you are trustworthy? If so, that becomes part of the process that you engage in. Always be mindful that fear plays a big role in a negotiation. To what degree can you use it to affect the negotiation?

Be aware of the impression you wish to create. Do you want to leave that person believing I'm no one to be trifled with or I'm someone who can be trusted or I'm someone who is kind? Or I'm someone who wants the best for both of us? Consider how you wish to leave the negotiation. In so doing, play your role as you're entering into and engaging in the negotiation.

Chapter 6

✦ ✦ ✦ ✦ ✦ ✦ ✦ ✦ ✦ ✦ ✦ ✦

Triggers: *Discovering the Hot Buttons that Stimulate Emotions*

Allen Carter ushered his opponent, Terrence Titler, into the private dining room at his exclusive club room at the racetrack. As the waiter hovered over them, Allen ordered an expensive bottle of wine and said, "Terrence, feel free to order anything you like." At every opportunity, Allen exuded an air of wealth.

Terrence came to the meeting with the intent of buying Allen's racehorse. Terrence's business was shaky, but he believed that he would attract more clients if he owned a racehorse. He knew that once he had a horse, he would be welcome in the rarified world of horse racing. Surely, business would improve once he was part of that set.

At the conclusion of the meal, Allen and Terrence began negotiating the price of the horse. Allen allowed a hint of condescension to creep into his voice. "Of course you know, Terrence, taking care of a horse involves feed, training, and vet bills. Are you *sure* you are prepared for the expense?" As Terrence sat up straighter, he took a deep breath and said, "Absolutely! It will be no problem at all." He then made an offer for the horse that was more than he could afford, but with that kind of challenge, how could he back down?

Personality Traits

Terrence and Allen displayed common personality traits. People generally display characteristics of one of four personality types. Knowing this directly affects the way you negotiate. The four personality types are coordinator, investigator, trendsetter, and relater.

The *coordinator* is an organized, passionate, creative, and motivated person. She is calm and flexible, someone who likes to have fun.

The *investigator* is intense. She's more cerebral than intuitive. She also relies more heavily on her perceptive skills. The investigator tends to have somewhat of an innovative mind-set. These individuals tend to be very secretive and somewhat isolated and cautious about trusting someone.

The *trendsetter* is social, charming, energetic, and comfortable in almost any situation in which she finds herself. If she is not comfortable, she seeks ways to increase her comfort. This is a person you'll see happily networking in a social situation; she makes connections very easily. She is outgoing and radiates attractiveness while admiring others and easily adapting to new environments. She is easily able to influence others.

The *relater* is a problem solver. She is self-motivated, engaging, honest, and has a high level of integrity. The relater has the tenacity to get the job done. This individual is detail oriented and builds connections within networks, paying attention to the power people.

Anyone can shift among the four personality traits based on their needs and the situation. Terrence wanted to buy Allen's horse; he was projecting the position of a relator. He wanted to build connections to power people within the racetrack world. He was motivated to improve his business. He was engaging with Allen because he determined he was going to get Allen to sell him the horse because of how the horse would be a benefit to his overall business activities.

Allen was displaying the traits of a trendsetter; he was social; the racetrack was *his* world. He had to be somewhat charming and display energy so that Terrence would feel comfortable with him.

Triggers

Allen allowed a hint of condescension to creep into his voice when he asked, "Of course you know, Terrence, taking care of a horse involves feed, training, and vet bills. Are you *sure* you are prepared for the expense?" This question served as a trigger in provoking a reaction out of Terrence. Allen was eliciting any type of body language gesture that might reveal if Terrence was somewhat uneasy about the money he would need to spend on the horse. Allen's positioning provoked a trigger that would do two things: First, it would make Terrence somewhat uneasy as he contemplated, "How much is this going to cost?" At the same time, from a negotiation perspective, he was setting Terrence up for the expectation that buying the horse was going to cost a lot more than he might be willing to spend. The implicit challenge was, "Are you man enough?" (This specific challenge has caused people to undertake all kinds of risk, from smart to foolhardy.) Nevertheless, it's an excellent way to position yourself at the beginning of a negotiation. By watching the body language response of the opposing negotiator, you gain insight into what he thinks of your attempts to position him.

Allen created an environment to underscore the challenge to Terrence's manhood. He held the negotiation in an extremely upscale environment because he recognized Terrence's craving to improve his status. The positioning was designed to set up Terrence to pay more for the horse than he planned. Imagine the same conversation in the stable surrounded by horse manure.

Purpose of Triggers

Triggers are a way to invoke a mind-set in the other negotiator so that you can manipulate him into an advantageous position for yourself. Therefore you need to understand the value of triggers and to what degree you use them. Allen used a trigger with Terrence of stressing the cost of owning a horse. That challenged Terrence's ego and the image he wanted to project. The negotiation became a matter of saving face.

When I was a teenager, my friend dared me to speak to girls our age. That was a challenge, a trigger, to make me say, "I accept your challenge." Triggers are used in a lot of situations to test others or change their mind-set about how they might do something.

Triggers versus Hot Buttons

Hot buttons are situations that I define as those that may make somebody lose control, and thus are dangerous. As an example,

I used to get very angry if someone cut in front of me when I was a younger driver. The trigger is being cut off. The hot button is the reaction of getting angry. Suppose you were raised to believe that it is rude to interrupt another person who is talking. Imagine yourself engaged in a negotiation where you have a lot at stake. Your irritation is growing because of the many obstacles in your path. You feel your irritation turn to anger. Then your opponent interrupts you. The trigger of being interrupted sets off the hot button reaction.

Sometimes triggers will invoke hot buttons. Here's the point of the usefulness of triggers and hot buttons: You may use triggers to manipulate someone's hot button. Then you know how to control them mentally. Allen used a trigger of discussing the cost of the horse's care to hit Terrence's hot button of wanting to be a man with an air of success.

Look for the effectiveness of triggers by reading body language. Is the other negotiator tugging at his collar? You now know there's a trigger at work. Watch body language to gain valuable insight by understanding the other negotiator's mindset, motivation, and the trigger that provokes a hot button. You can then invoke that trigger to cause the same reaction later in the negotiation.

Negotiation Triggers

Allen taunted Terrence to make sure that he would step up to the challenge of owning a horse. There are other negotiation triggers: fear, anger, desire to be comfortable, desire to be trusted, complacency, and the threat of loss. There are many more triggers depending upon the type of individual that you're dealing with.

Once you understand the person's motivation, you know how to manipulate the situation and which triggers and hot buttons to use.

Suppose your opponent values being comfortable. As we've discussed in a previous chapter, the limbic system is focused on maintaining comfort. Create discomfort through triggers to stimulate the other person to seek comfort. You can use a trigger to keep him in that uncomfortable state for as long as that purpose serves you. Then allow him to escape that environment to a more comfortable one so that he is rewarded for making concessions. Remember how in Chapter 3 I discussed using the temperature of a room to make people uncomfortable?

Consider the power of urgency as a trigger. For example, Norman and Vivian were both interested in buying a property. They got into a bidding war with each other. The real estate agent was in the middle between the two people. He said, "I need to have your decision by 5:00 today because I have another person who's put in a bid for this house. I'm not allowed to tell you what that amount is, so come up with your best offer."

Urgency in this case served as a trigger, but only to the degree that the opposing party believed it to be. I'm making a distinction about the usage of triggers, especially as it relates to urgency in this particular case. Norman thought, "Okay, let's see what happens. I'm not going to move. I'm not going to budge at all." Vivian raised her offer, which the owner accepted. Norman lost the deal and realized, "The next time this real estate agent says something about there being a sense of urgency (the trigger), I better believe it."

Use the wrong trigger at the wrong time and you can get penalized. As an example, in the situation mentioned with Norman and Vivian, the trigger of urgency and time was used to entice both to make a better offer. The trigger worked with Vivian and thus she increased her offer. Norman didn't believe the urgency that was being invoked and made no movement. With Vivian, the sense of urgency was the right trigger used at the right time; for Norman, because he didn't necessarily believe there was another offer, it was the wrong trigger at the wrong time.

Always be aware of the situation in which you use triggers. Plan how to use triggers at specific points in the negotiation to have the best-possible outcomes.

Triggers with Personality Types

Personalities will respond differently to triggers. Consider the real estate deal Vivian won. Vivian was a *coordinator*. She responded well to the trigger of urgency. Coordinators are passionate, creative, calm, and usually flexible. The sense of urgency might disrupt the calmness that person will normally feel in any environment. Vivian really wanted that property and was unsettled at the chance she might lose the deal. She quickly moved to revise her offer because she became uncomfortable with the idea of losing. The trigger of urgency moved her into action.

Consider how the *investigator* might react to urgency. That type of person is someone who is somewhat secretive, isolated, and intense. Norman was an investigator. He needed concrete information—proof that the counteroffer was real. The real estate agent used the same trigger, the sense of urgency, with this individual. Norman thought, "Is the agent trying to manipulate me? I bet there is no other buyer. Let me see what happens." Urgency had no effect on him. Know the triggers that work with personality types; know when to apply them.

The hot button for the coordinator is disruption of her calmness. That person is not going to feel comfortable in a situation with a sense of urgency that you've invoked. She likes to stay in a calm environment. Suppose the coordinator-type person sat in front of you. You might observe body language revealing her discomfort: rubbing her hands to comfort herself, fidget, or play with objects in the room. She will tell you through these actions about her level of comfort. Your role is to guide the other person to feel a level of discomfort so you can guide her toward comfort. If you were in the role of real estate agent, you'd say, "You will be more comfortable and increase the chance of getting this property if you make your best offer." Influence your opponent through skillful use of hot buttons and triggers. They'll direct you to know exactly how to assist her in achieving what she wants.

Vivian is a *trendsetter*. You should display a lot of energy because that's the trendsetter's preferred environment. She senses a subliminal message based on your level of energy. You might say, "You really should increase your offer right now if you want to get this property" instead of the lower-key message, "Maybe you might think about upping your offer if you really want to get this property."

The reason I stress the level of energy is to emphasize the trigger of your tone—the pace and volume of your speech. Use it to convey the level of energy that you have and connect with the personality type of the person to whom you are speaking. Don't use the same level of energy with an *investigator*. Remember, he's already secretive; high energy scares him. He may back off in fear, wondering, "What is this person really trying to do? Why is she trying to rush me?" His personality type becomes a little more skeptical and thus you would not want to use high energy in such a situation.

When Personality Types Team Up

Barry and Kaitlyn Samples leased cars from the same dealer for over 20 years. Their pattern was to sign three-year leases and to turn the car over at the end of that period. After they moved out of state, their car lease was up so they approached a dealer in their new town to turn in the leased car and obtain a new model. After signing all the paperwork, Kaitlyn picked up the new car. She grimaced when she drove out of the lot—the car was missing an important safety feature on which she relied to avoid collisions. "I was sure Barry asked for that," she thought. She called the dealer when she got home and said she needed to switch the car for one with the feature. Boyd McCormick, the manager of the car dealership, said, "I don't think I can do that. Let me check." He called Kaitlyn back and said, "I talked to the Finance Division. They said once you signed the paperwork, you committed to taking that car."

Kaitlyn was a *relator,* a problem solver with a lot of social connections. She would not accept "no" as an answer. She called the Finance Division, who knew nothing about the problem Kaitlyn described. Barry got involved. He was an *investigator*—a person who was cautious about trusting the general manager. Barry called the North American headquarters of the car manufacturer. After describing his long history of leasing cars made by the automobile manufacturer, he received an apology for what occurred. Next, Barry called Boyd. The manager was very friendly, called him by his first name, but still balked at switching the car. Barry discussed the calls he had made and finished with, "You know my wife is big into social media," and he paused. Boyd was silent for a moment, and then said, "Mr. Samples, we'll take care of switching the car. Please tell your wife to share on social media that we did what was necessary in order to satisfy your needs." The couple got the car they wanted.

What were the factors that led to this outcome? Barry's investigator personality resulted in him doing his homework and using the chain of command within the car company to get to the top. He was suspicious about why the dealership manager would not change cars. As he listened to the manager attempt to deflect his wish for a different car, he found out Boyd did not want to accept the car back because it was not a commonly leased car model. Boyd said he did not want to get stuck with it. Barry concluded the story about the Finance Division was just that—a story. He held this conclusion back.

When Barry confronted Boyd with the phone calls he made, he showed he did his homework and put Boyd on guard. Barry activated Boyd's trigger that said, "Uh-oh, I've been caught." That also pressed an invisible hot button in him that cried, "How do I extract myself from this situation? I have to save face." Barry then applied more pressure to him with the statement, "My wife is very active in social media," meaning "If you give me a raw deal, others will hear about it."

Boyd was a coordinator. He was organized and motivated, usually calm. He wanted to solve the problem and make Barry stop complaining so calm would be restored. He realized, "I have a serious situation. How do I really get out of it and do so as gracefully as possible?"

Note that Boyd switched from calling Barry by his first name to his last name. The transformation indicated he had a different level of respect for Barry. There is a nonverbal display of respect when somebody formalizes any situation. It's also somewhat like watching a change in body language. If you were looking at Boyd talking to Barry on the phone, you would have seen him sit up straighter, paying more attention. The coordinator personality was fearful of the storm that would follow a complaint on social media.

Was there any value in a direct confrontation with Boyd? Barry could have said, "You lied about talking to the Finance Division." This accusation would have pushed Boyd's hot button to create an uncomfortable environment until Boyd agreed to give Barry and Kaitlyn the car they wanted. However, Boyd agreed to switch cars without Barry needing to accuse him of lying. Barry knew he needed Boyd in the future, since he ran the only car dealership of this kind in the town.

If this discussion took place in person instead of over the phone, Barry would have paused and allowed Boyd to squirm until he gave in. Then Barry would have smiled, a nonverbal signal that indicated, "Thanks for agreeing to see things more my way."

Boyd displayed his coordinator personality when he became calmer. He used creativity and diligence to locate the car the Samples wanted. He was motivated to resolve the issue. The Samples could have asked for more concessions as a result of the discomfort they experienced in going through the ordeal they had to endure to investigate the situation. Boyd would likely have been amenable to requests. If he said no, the Samples could have started the whole cycle again of putting him back into a state of discomfort. By doing so, they would have gone through the process until he said, "I'll give you whatever you want to comfort you."

Although Boyd gave the Samples what they wanted, he was not finished with the negotiation and was still unhappy at having to accept the original car back. A few days after the agreement about the swap, Barry stopped by the dealership to get the new car. Boyd told him, "If you spend only $15 more per month, over a six-year period of time you could buy this car." Boyd's hot button was trying to avoid getting stuck with the car. He was doing whatever he could to protect his position; the Samples were doing the same. Barry probed Boyd's motives by saying, "Wait a minute. Whose interests are you considering here—ours or yours? It sounds like you're just trying to position this deal such that you don't get this car back. All you are concerned about is getting rid of the car. You are not concerned about my wishes at all. Is that what I'm to take away from this discussion, that you are not interested in my safety or what I want? Is this how your dealership deals with customers?"

Note how Barry used a trigger to make Boyd uncomfortable. Barry watched Boyd's body language. Boyd placed a hand over his eyes. His body language said, "I don't want to see this situation." Then he covered his ear, indicating, "I don't want to hear any more about it." As he turned his head sideways, he was conveying, "I'm not going to take this on head on."

If you're talking on the phone to the other negotiator, listen to his voice to detect changes in inflection. You will gain insight as to whether a trigger is starting to lead to a hot button. Imagine the other negotiator saying to himself, "I'm going in the wrong direction again. Let me see how I can give him whatever he wants so I can get out of this uncomfortable situation."

Use the power of probing to find out if a trigger will activate a hot button and cause discomfort. In so doing you get a lot more out of the negotiation. Keep applying pressure to cause more discomfort. Barry followed the subtle threat of "My wife is very big in the social media space" with a pause. He did not have to spell out the implication: "Treat me wrong if you want to, but a lot of people will hear about it." The YouTube video of 2010, "United Breaks Guitars," is an example of the power of social media, with over 15.5 million views, and undoubtedly caused United Airlines a lot of embarrassment.

Always know before you enter a negotiation how you can use triggers and hot buttons. Do your homework to find out about the person to whom you're going to apply these strategies so you have a plan. Anticipate what you are going to do, how you're going to implement certain aspects of your plan, and how you are going to maneuver around potential roadblocks. Definitely consider the use of triggers and hot buttons before you even get anywhere near the negotiation table.

Identifying the Personality Type of the Other Negotiator

Earlier in this chapter I identified the four personality types. How do you confirm which personality type you are dealing with when you are talking to the opposing negotiator? People switch back and forth between personality types all the time dependent upon how they feel, the situation that they're in, and the level of comfort they're experiencing. The coordinator can change to the investigator type, which can change to the trendsetter type, which can change to a relater type. One of the things that you do is to probe to see what characteristics are predominant during any point; use a trigger to invoke yet a different personality type.

Suppose you said in a jovial manner at the onset of a negotiation, "This is going to be a great experience today. Wouldn't you agree?" The coordinator is calm, passionate, creative, and flexible. She likes to have fun. The coordinator will agree with you.

Let's say you said the same thing in the same tone to a person you suspect is an investigator. That person is somewhat secretive and isolated. He thinks, "What is with all this happiness and gaiety? I need to find out what he is really up to and trying to do before I allow him in my space." Watch the body language of the investigator as he sits with arms crossed and says, in a guarded manner. "Sure, it will be fun." Remember, the body never lies. Pay attention to the crossed arms and defensive manner.

Expect the trendsetter to be more engaged and open to having such an interaction. Make her comfortable. Stress the social aspects of the discussion you are engaging her in, and offer her some networking opportunity as a reward after the negotiation is completed.

Observe for problem-solving skills in the relator. This person loves to solve problems and has a high level of integrity. If you accidentally misstate something during a negotiation, expect the relator to correct you, even if it is detrimental to her position.

Body Language to Stimulate Triggers

How do you use the tone of your voice and the pace to enhance a negotiation so that you're achieving your outcomes? I walked into a store and wanted an item that was no longer on sale (it had ended two days before). I said to the salesperson, named Damian, "I would like to have this item." Damian said, "No problem, sir." Then I said, "I'd like to have it at the price it was listed for a few days ago." Damian replied, "Sir, that sale ended." I said leaning in toward him, "Yes, but you have the authority to give me that at the sales price, right?"

I used body language to nod my head in the affirmative, trying to get that person to follow me. I used tonality when I lowered my voice and also used the implied trigger of, "You are important." That was the hidden meaning behind my words. Damian said, "No sir, actually I can't give it to you at that price." "Okay," I replied and then I stepped forward. Again in that confident voice, leaning toward him, I inquired, "Why can't you give it to me?" Damian responded, "Sir, I'm just not allowed to."

Here's a negotiation tactic that you always need to employ when you're seeking something. If someone says he can't get it for you, you communicate the assumption that *somebody* can. Thus I said in the same type of voice, "*Who* can?" Damian said, "If anybody, my manager can." I said, "May I please speak to your manager?" I said that with a higher sense of authority in my voice. I was using tonality to indicate I'm somebody to be reckoned with as opposed to "Oh okay, well may I please speak to the manager?" I knew this individual would go back to his manager.

Damian went to the back of the store and said to Noel, his manager, "There's a crazy guy out front. He wants this item at the price it was on sale for a few days ago and I told him I can't do it." Noel replied, "Why are you coming to me?" Damian admitted, "I told him you might be able to help him." Rolling his eyes, Noel sighed and walked to the front of the store. In a dismissive tone, he said to me, "Sir, the sale ended several days ago."

I replied, "So you mean to tell me that *you* are not empowered to satisfy a customer." I exactly matched his tone. This invoked a trigger: "He is just like me. People tend to like people who are like themselves. By matching his tonality I set off the trigger that he likely was not even aware of that conveyed: "Okay, this guy and I are on the same page."

Here's another tactic I employed when he made the statement that the sale had already ended. I challenged him and that was the trigger that I invoked in him. Here he was standing in front of his employee and made to appear to be belittled because he did not have the power to satisfy me. I took note of the fact that Damian looked at Noel in a side glance, meaning "*You* really don't have that level of power?"

Remember, I used the trigger of "Are you powerless?" which also pressed a hot button in Noel to say "Wait a minute. I've got to stand up for my manhood in front of my employee." The manager capitulated by responding, "Of course I can give you this at the sales price." That's the way you could use your tone and pace to enhance your message.

The four personality types respond differently to tone and pace of messages. For example, think of the coordinator as a person who is organized, motivated, passionate, creative, calm, and flexible, and likes to have fun. With the coordinator type, you may start the negotiation by saying, "This is going to be so much fun. When we reach this agreement we are going to have so much fun. We will remember it for a lifetime. I'll tell you something else, it's going to allow us to be more creative with the way we craft the outcome of this experience. If we have to be flexible in so doing, I'm sure that you and I together can truly handle it."

What message have I just shared? I used certain words that resonate with the traits of the individual that reinforce the fact that I'm aligned with the way this person thinks. Remember what I shared earlier: People like people who are like themselves. At the same time, I've reassured this individual without threatening her that things are going to work out well because we'll be flexible. We will adapt to any changes that come up.

Can you imagine the tone of voice I used in that message? If you are thinking "upbeat," you are right. My voice was light-hearted, friendly, and enthusiastic when I talked about the fun of the negotiation. I did not convey that the negotiation would be serious, demanding, or upsetting. The coordinator wants to be calm. If you get too excited and get her too excited, you can put her in a state of discomfort. Be cautious in keeping a balance between fun and excitement.

Reckoning with Your Own Triggers and Hot Buttons

So far I have shared how you can use the other negotiator's hot buttons and triggers. The astute negotiator is also observing how you react. What are your triggers and hot buttons? How do you respond when the other negotiator is honing in on your own triggers and hot buttons, and is attempting to control the negotiation by using them?

Know your triggers and hot buttons. For example,

- Do you believe you should always get the best possible deal? (Have you ever seen a person who is so focused on saving money that he drives 20 minutes to return batteries to a store because he found them somewhere else for 2 cents less? I have.)
- Do you believe that for every negotiation there has to be a clear winner and clear loser?

- Do you find that when other people make certain assumptions about you based on the way you look, you react to set them straight?
- Is dismissiveness or condescension a hot button that makes you fight back?
- Do you get angry when you are interrupted?
- Do you get angry when you feel your time is being wasted?
- Does being put on hold for several long minutes make you angry even before your phone call negotiation begins?

Earlier in this chapter I shared that other drivers cutting me off activated my hot button and made me angry. Realizing I would react in such a situation, I knew not to let that trigger cause me to react in that manner. I had to become aware of it and want to change my behavior.

Knowing that the other negotiator will use some of your hot buttons and triggers against you means heightening your awareness and preparing how you're going to react in such situations. Consider reacting in the opposite manner than the negotiator expects. This will throw her off and disrupt what she planned to do in the negotiation. The investigator will be suspicious about why you gave an unexpected response. "What's he trying to pull off?" he'll wonder. The relator will go into problem-solving mode while the trendsetter will be uncomfortable with your response and will strive to become more comfortable. The flexible coordinator will likely be most successful in dealing with your unexpected response.

Giving unexpected responses is one way to combat the other negotiator's usage of your triggers against you. At the same time, use a trigger against her while she's in a state of confusion wondering why you did not act the way that you were supposed to. Confront the issue head on: "Why did you think I'd act like that?" Say it in a condescending manner, pushing her back on her proverbial heels. When she responds with, "Oh I didn't mean anything by it," you reply: "Oh, yes you did." Your voice would display the mild antagonism taking on the traits of a somewhat secretive investigator. What does she do next?

- Does she back down as you become more intense?
- Does she appear to stumble in her pace?
- Does she make more concessions?
- How does her body language change?

Observe your opponent's body language, tone, and pace to determine to what degree your behavior is helping you achieve the goal of the negotiation. But even moreso, control her use of triggers against you and the hot button issues that she thought would cause you to react in a certain way. Sometimes, a strong offense weakens a strong defense.

Now take note. I said before that you should always know what those triggers and hot buttons are. Be aware that negotiators use red herrings. These are items in a negotiation that have the appearance of value but you are willing to forego in order to achieve something else. Red herrings have little value to you but great perceived value to the other negotiator. Use them to trigger the "I want it" factor in the other negotiator, which becomes nothing more than a trigger to cause her to salivate at the thought of quenching her desire. Be on guard for the red herrings that others offer you; don't get deflected by them.

In Summary

Develop a keen understanding of the priorities in a negotiation. What do you want out of it? What triggers do you need to use to achieve those goals? What body language signals do you anticipate you and your opponent will use?

Look at the best- and worst-case scenarios. By having those outcomes in mind you will understand where you are at any one point in the negotiation based on the body language signals that you've actually received. Observe reactions to triggers—do they enhance or impede the negotiation? Use them to get more of what you want. To the degree they don't, toss them aside.

Always understand what triggers will likely help you gain. What are the hot buttons and triggers, and why do they work? What are your alternatives if the hot buttons are not effective? How are the personality types likely to react to a trigger? How can you thwart others using your hot buttons? Have plans in place for how you're going to react based on the triggers that are used against you in a negotiation. Observe the impact of triggers on body language. You will literally be able to hone in on the actions that occur based on the triggers you use and the hot buttons that are invoked. With this knowledge you have a better chance of enhancing the overall flow of the negotiation and enhancing the probability that you'll come out ahead in the negotiation.

Chapter 7

* * * * * * * * * * * *

Nodes: *Appreciating the Affinity Principle*

The meeting began with what seemed like idle chatter. Toby skillfully interviewed Clarise as he probed into her education and work experience. At every outset, Toby looked for common ground. "I went to that college, too," he exclaimed. "Why, I live in that development also." "You're a Cubs fan too?" Prior to the meeting, Toby spent time on social media researching Clarise. None of the details she supplied were new to him. Toby leaned forward as Clarise leaned forward, and carefully mimicked her body language. After 10 minutes of conversation, Clarise said, "I can't believe how much we have in common!" Toby masked his grin.

What Are Nodes?

Nodes are personality types. There are four types: hard, easy, closed, and open. Refer to Figure 7.1. When it comes to negotiation and reading body language, consider the nodes from four different perspectives. The hard negotiator is opposite from an easygoing negotiator. The hard person is the north axis. The easy person is at the south axis. On the west/east axis the closed personality type is opposite from the open personality–type negotiator.

The Negotiation Nodes

Negotiator Personality Types

Hard
(Can present challenging negotiation)

Hard & Closed
I'll tell you my best offer and you can take it or leave it. (Impression) I don't care about you!

Hard & Open
There's not really a lot you can say to make me alter my perspective but I'll listen to you.

Closed
(Cautious about sharing information and possibly concerned about being taken advantage of.)

Open
(Initially trusting – believes people are good and no one sets out to hurt you.)

Easy & Closed
I'm cautious and apprehensive but I'm willing to see where this will go.

Easy & Open
I'll follow your lead because I trust you.

Easy
(willing to go along to get along. Doesn't believe anything should be hidden (i.e. lay your cards on the table)

© Greg Williams,
The Master Negotiator &
Body Language Expert

You're always negotiating!

www.TheMasterNegotiator.com

Want more insightful information for free ...
Go to www.TheMasterNegotiator.com
Click on 'Blog'. Click on 'About Greg' to sign up
and receive more insightful information weekly.

Overview of the Nodes

A hard negotiator is the person who says, "I'll tell you my best offer. Take it or leave it." The hard is a strident person who projects indifference about the needs or positions of the opponent. This type of personality attempts to dominate the negotiation, resulting in a challenging negotiation. Hard negotiators are motivated to win, sometimes at all costs.

The easy personality type is someone who is willing to go along to get along. The easy negotiators are optimistic, don't believe anything should be hidden, and are willing to lay their cards on the table. Their goal is to achieve an agreement that will make everyone happy. The hard negotiator is more apt to take advantage of the easy personality.

The closed personality is someone who is cautious about sharing information. These people are paranoid about being exploited and need reassurance that their interests will not be harmed. Envision the closed person as a turtle hiding in a shell. He needs to be convinced to come out of his shell. You can quickly drive the closed personalities back into their shell if they perceive that you're trying to take advantage of them. That will serve as confirmation of their concerns that the world is out to get them.

The open personality type is initially trusting. This person's behavior conveys, "I'm not closed. I'm not very easy. I'm not very hard. I'm willing to see exactly what will happen." The open personality has the perception people are good until proven otherwise. You will receive the open personality's trust, but at the first opportunity he senses he needs to be reserved or protective of himself, he can become the exact opposite of open, which would be closed.

"Birds of a Feather Flock Together"

The expression "birds of a feather flock together" in the negotiation context means people like people who are like themselves. From a negotiation perspective, you will find people build rapport more quickly with others with whom they feel an affinity. You relate most easily to people who think and react like you do. You recognize yourself in the opponent.

Two people who are of the easy personality type may find it simple to negotiate with each other. But two hard negotiators may butt heads and get mired in impasses. One of them may need to switch nodes in order to use effective strategies and tactics to reach agreement. That's why it's important to understand what node you're negotiating against and what node you're being perceived as having. To the degree that people sense you are like them and that turns out to be favorable, you can use that as an advantage during the negotiation.

At the beginning of this chapter, you read how Toby researched Clarise to find their commonalities. Toby deliberately used the affinity principle to frame the negotiation to encourage Clarise to be more trusting, to be led simply because she liked Toby. A lot of people overlook the power of establishing affinity and likeability. Some opponents will make concessions that they normally would not make simply because they have an affinity for their opponent. Use your awareness of the affinity principle when dealing with someone with whom you have an affinity. Be aware you may have a predisposition to easily give in during a negotiation if you feel an affinity toward your opponent.

When jurors are asked to make judgments and decisions about awarding money to people who are claiming they have been injured or have been wronged in some way, the affinity principle applies during the decision-making process. A trial is like a negotiation with attorneys making offers and counteroffers, positioning themselves, and using strategies to be persuasive and to convince someone to do something that they want them to do. Attorneys use strategies to sway the jurors to their perspective. Jurors have to feel the plaintiff is just like them in order to want to award money.

As an example, someone on a property was chopping down a tree. As a result of his technique, the tree fell the wrong way and hit his neighbor, Quinton, paralyzing him. Imagine you are in court. Quinton is on the witness stand. He says, "All I was doing was just sitting around. I was drinking some beer and all of a sudden the next thing I know here comes this big-ass tree falling on me. It paralyzed me."

Since the jurors don't use such language, the plaintiff is distancing himself from them. Suppose Quinton said, "My wife and I were just sitting in the front yard looking at the sunset. My daughter had just called to me and said, 'Dad, are you going to help me with my homework?'" Quinton painted a picture of having a loving family. Further, he testifies, "The next thing I know a tree comes crashing into my front yard. Fortunately, I was able to push my wife out of the way to keep her from being hit, but it struck me. It left me in the position that I'm in today."

Now Quinton shows he has values, he is loving, and self-sacrificing. The jurors think, "Wow, that could have been me." As soon as the people in the jury start to think that, the affinity perspective has crystallized. Quinton has established a commonality with the jury and is more likely to get a higher verdict with this testimony than if he had testified as I described in the first example.

Establishing Affinity

Let's say you are a speaker seeking to get hired by a corporation to do some training for the employees. You use a wide variety of research tools to gather information about the corporation and the person who will make the hiring decision.

One thing that you can consider is the process through which this individual hired speakers in the past. This insight gives you information about the buying process. For example, you may find out the hiring person wants to hire a speaker who

- likes to tell stories during the course of the presentation,
- is easy to work with, and
- shows up early or stays late.

Now you know what the hiring person is looking for. Find out what the individual and corporation value. When you're speaking to that individual use her words and address the values that go into the process of determining which speaker she is going to hire.

You may wonder, "How do I go about gathering this information?" Use the Internet, YouTube, LinkedIn, and Facebook to do some background research on the individual. You may find out where the person went to school if you go to LinkedIn, how long she has been in her position, and about her prior work experience.

Build on these facts to build rapport. As you do so, listen to the way she responds. Try to speak at the same pace; use words similar to the ones she uses. This sends a subliminal message: "I'm a lot like you." The hiring person finds herself thinking, "He's like me. He speaks and sounds like me." You're building rapport based on the node type that you are projecting. In identifying her past activities and projecting an image that's similar to hers, subliminally you're influencing her. By recognizing her node type and replicating that, you're increasing your likeability factor with her, which creates more rapport at a faster pace.

That level of rapport should transfer into an easier negotiation for the two of you.

Body Language: Revealing the Node

Body language reveals your opponent's node. For example, your adversary, Vincent Dessin, projects a hard style. You lean toward Vincent with a broad smile on your face. You've done some research; you find out Vincent went to Penn State. You say to Vincent, "You went to Penn State. I went to Penn State, too." A glance at Vincent's face shows he is stone-faced. He has given you no feedback. You say to yourself, "I should have gotten a reaction from that. Maybe he did not like his college experience. Or maybe he is a hard-nosed negotiator."

Based on your research, you already have some insight about Vincent's negotiation personality. You carry it a step further. "I understand you majored in finance at Penn State." This time you've positioned your body so you are halfway between leaning back and leaning forward. Vincent does not react. As you literally lean all the way back in your chair you say, "I guess you had the same reaction I had when I went to Penn State." Vincent says, "What was that reaction?" You realize that by you leaning back away from Vincent he has told you he doesn't want you too close. Vincent is not there to make friends. He wants to get down to business. You can even state that. Say, "So let's get down to business" as you lower the tone of your voice. You might gently place your hand on the table to say, "Let's start this process." Your opponent's reactions to your body language will give you insight.

Contrast that to the easy negotiator, Girija Nair. You use the same tactics. You say, "Oh you went to Penn State. I went to Penn State, too." You're leaning forward. You observe as Girija all of a sudden leans forward and gives you that big broad smile also. Two things have happened. Number one, Girija has indicated, "I recognize and like the fact there's commonality between the two of us." You leaned forward. You smiled. She leans forward and smiles, meaning you are leading her. This is another signal that Girija might be an easygoing negotiator.

If you have misinterpreted the easy node signals, at worst you would assess Girija as an open personality-type negotiator. She is saying, "I'm trusting and you're allowing me to build more trust just based on this short interaction you and I are having."

In the opening scenario of this chapter I shared an insight about body language with Toby mimicking Clarise's body language. When she leaned forward, he leaned forward. Mimicking body language is useful to building rapport. In the example of the easy negotiator, you leaned forward and that person leaned forward; you smiled and that person smiled. You are building rapport and leading the person. There's an intrinsic value in building a rapport, meaning people like people who are like themselves.

Recognizing the Negotiator's Node

Scott Sherman believed he was at the top of his game as a busy plaintiff trial attorney. His office took big cases and won big. Feeling the need to get some additional consulting services, Scott invited a prominent consultant, Francine Farley, to his office to meet with him and an associate. "Bring a sample work product," he told her.

Scott sat at the head of the conference room, leaning back in his chair. Scott was about six feet tall and lanky. Francine sat to his left; Scott's junior associate, Helen, sat across the table from Francine. The associate sat leaning forward while she examined Francine's sample report. When Scott glanced at the report, he spotted something he did not like. "This is sophomoric. Look at these illustrations." Francine pulled back and wondered, "Why is he insulting me like this?"

Then Scott sneered at Francine as he said, "How much do your services cost? Everybody wants to put their hands in my pocket. I worked with another consultant of your type and was not happy with what she did. I wanted to sue her but found out she had no assets."

While Scott got called away to take a phone call, his associate said to Francine, "I really like your report. I think you did a great job." When Scott returned to the room, they concluded the meeting with the plan that Francine would get back to him and give him a proposal.

Francine drove away; she had trouble driving due to her headache. She thought, "My body is telling me something about this experience." Deciding she needed more information about Scott, she called colleagues who knew him. Her discussions with colleagues revealed Scott was suspected of having a cocaine habit and an erratic personality; he was nice one moment and screaming the next. He also had a bad payment history. This information reinforced Francine's decision that she did not need him as a client. She wrote him a letter saying she was too busy to take on the cases in his practice. After that she and Scott avoided each other whenever they had an opportunity.

What happened here?

Scott made no attempt to build rapport with Francine as he projected himself as a hard negotiator. His body language of leaning back in his chair confirmed this, as well as sounding strident and hostile. He was trying to project an image of someone that Francine did not want to mess with. Francine was an open negotiator, who withdrew into a closed node when she was attacked.

At the meeting, Helen displayed an open body language and spoke in a consoling, apologetic manner with a soft tone. She had her arms apart as though she was welcoming Francine to come closer. The associate played good cop/bad cop with Francine: she waited until Scott was out of the room to express her opinions about the quality of Francine's report. Although she said nothing disparaging about her boss, her actions and words conveyed she had a different opinion.

Instead of retreating into the closed node, Francine might have matched Scott's tone and body language and challenged his attacks on her work product: "Why would you say this is sophomoric?" Obviously, he thought he was in control.

In this scenario, Francine had the courage to stand up for herself and state what she was feeling. "I sense hostility coming from you based on your body language, the aggressiveness in your tone, the words you are using, your gestures, and finger pointing." Honesty pays. Had Scott responded by saying "Damn straight!" Francine could have said, "Thank you," gotten up and left the office. She would have been saying, "No one talks to me in such a manner; I don't need you or your business that badly . . . have a nice day." If on the other hand Francine accepted Scott's demeanor, she would have been setting herself up for more of the same. Remember, you're always negotiating. That which you do today influences tomorrow's negotiations.

When you try to build rapport and it is not working, first consider that your opponent may be a hostile, hard negotiator. Perhaps you need to back off and take a different approach. Be careful that you do not overreach or do anything dishonest to establish rapport. For example, Lucy said to Penny, "Oh, you went to Kansas State. I did too. I majored in business." Lucy was lying about her background in an attempt to reach out to Penny. In response, Penny said, "I majored in business, too. Who was your favorite professor?" When Lucy could not supply a name, Penny realized Lucy was lying. Lucy harmed herself and proved she was untrustworthy and a phony. This would confirm the closed negotiator's belief that Lucy was out to trick her. Penny said to herself, "I better go further into my shell now because Lucy has already shown me that she's not trustworthy. She will lie to try to get me to do what she wants to manipulate me into a negotiation position."

Be careful to what degree you try to establish rapport with someone. In today's environment of instant fact checking and the importance of integrity in interacting with others, be mindful of the importance of being truthful. To do otherwise puts you at risk of being called out on lies and destroying your negotiation and reputation.

Recognize that your opponent will detect manipulative use of commonalities to create rapport. For example, New Yorker Louise Denton bought a house in another state. When she entered a furniture store, Tony Francesco, the salesman who waited on her exclaimed, "I'm from New York, too." As Louise reviewed her list of what she needed and wandered around the store, Tony kept close to her. In three hours he made five references to them both being New Yorkers, and even said, "We New Yorkers need to stick together." Louise noticed he thickened his New York accent as the morning wore on. Once Louise began finalizing her decisions, Tony knew the sale was assured. He dropped all references to being from New York.

The potential detriment of building rapport the way Tony did is the risk of coming across as a phony. Tony's ploy was transparent. Suppose after the sale was made when Louise and Tony discussed the timing of the furniture delivery, Tony switched out of the friendly, easy type of negotiator node. He would have risked antagonizing Louise and having her back out of the deal.

When you emphasize commonalities, make sure that you are being sincere and truthful. How would Louise have felt if she overheard Tony lying to the next customer who came into the store, "Oh, I am from Montana too"? Be genuine as opposed to pandering so your opponent doesn't think, "Now I see your real colors."

Building Rapport: Which Nodes Respond?

It is not always prudent to build rapport. The hard personality type may be suspicious if he detects you are making an effort to build rapport with him. He may view your attempts as insincere friendliness used to manipulate him. "Everybody should be friends" does not ring true for him. That's not part of his demeanor; he doesn't want any part of it. The hard node sees friendliness as a weakness. He may also start to consider you as being less competent. Remember, his personality type is one who says, "I'll tell you my best offer. I really don't care that much about you, so why in the world would you be trying to suck up to me?" This can lead to a more difficult negotiation because the hard node may get the perception once he makes an offer he can dig in his heels and not budge.

In response to this behavior, don't try to build rapport. Show this individual instead, "If you want to be hard-nosed, no problem. Bring it on. I can be just as hard-nosed as you are. By the way, if you want to mess with me, come on mess with me if you dare. We will get to an impasse. If *you* don't care, did I tell you that I was the inventor of not caring?"

Be careful of *how* and *when* you go about trying to build rapport. Consider how and if it will be beneficial. The *closed* negotiator needs a gentle approach to building rapport. Use quiet, calming speech and gestures. Don't make large gestures even from a body language perspective. You don't want to do anything that will excite that person or incite the closed negotiator to have the thought that you are out to hurt him.

With the *easy* negotiator the more rapport you build with her, the more she likes you. She wants to see that you're just like her. Make sure the negotiation goes down the path with everybody coming out ahead. The easy person wants everybody to be happy; you want to build rapport to show her that you can accomplish that goal with her.

With the *open* negotiator, send the message, "I know you're a trusting person; I'm a trusting person. We can get along together. If we happen to reach a potential impasse, we can solve this situation because you and I are like-minded. We are in this together."

Building a rapport in those situations with the closed, easy, and open personality types would be beneficial. The hard individual is someone you have to be very cautious as to what degree you even attempt to build rapport, if at all. The hard type of negotiator is one who doesn't care about touchy-feely approaches. If the person shakes your hand, he may even look at you sideways or look away from you to give you the message you really don't matter that much. Respond to his body language with your own hard body language.

One way to build rapport is to ask for your opponent's input. Ask him for his advice as to how he might handle a situation. He gives you his assessment. Then you can say to the degree that it matches what you wanted to hear or do anyway. "You know, that's a great idea. How about if we . . ." and you recite back to him what he said. That's a negotiation strategy tactic, but how can he disagree with that because it's his idea that you're feeding back to him? This is yet another way you can build rapport based on node types.

Varying the Personality or Node Type

Good negotiators may have to display all of these personality types during the course of the negotiation based on the opponent's negotiation type. The negotiating node may alter throughout the course of the negotiation. You might be in a negotiation with a person who your research showed was an easy negotiator. When that person displays hard behavior, you may need to switch to a hard approach personality type also.

You may need to switch from the node with which you are most comfortable and assume the characteristics of a different node. An individual who possesses the characteristics and personality type of an easy negotiator may need to play the role of a hard-nosed negotiator; this can be uncomfortable.

It may be to your strategic advantage to reflect the person's node. When you are reflective of an individual's personality type, that person sees you are more like him or her. As you progress through the negotiation, you can change. Be reflective to people's personality types so they see the actions that you commit as actions that they would commit.

Let's say you're in a room with an open-node negotiator. He's leaning forward, smiling at you attentively and then all of a sudden he pulls his body back to get as far away from you as possible. These signals show he has changed from an open to a hard or closed node and should cause you to reflect on what caused him to react that way.

Paul is a closed-node negotiator who is interacting with Yvonne. As Yvonne spoke, Paul leaned back, scowled, and retreated. Yvonne looked at him quizzically and said, "What just happened?" Paul replied, "What do you mean?" With that question Paul was seeking information about what Yvonne sensed or was trying to do. This guarded person was retreating into his shell.

Yvonne answered, "I just observed the fact that you seemed to withdraw." She gave him a hint that she could read his body language: "I just noticed that you sat back a moment ago or you've seem to have withdrawn." Paul explained, "I'm not sure to what degree the concession you just asked me to make is one that I can really give you. I don't know where that might take the negotiation." Yvonne asks, "Can you give me some insight as to how you might be able to assist us? We're in this together." Paul wants to feel safe and that Yvonne is not going to take advantage of him. Yvonne gives him the lead so he can feel comfortable.

Let's contrast that same reaction that I cited a moment ago with a hard-negotiator type. Andrea is a hard negotiator type negotiating with Ted. She thinks, "There's no way I'm going to make those concessions at all. This guy knows I really don't care anyway." Andrea is clicking her pen off and on as she leans back. What she's saying to Ted with this gesture is, "Let's get this thing over with. I don't even want to be bothered with this anymore."

Ted can ask the hard negotiator the same thing Yvonne posed to Paul, the closed negotiator. "What just happened?" Andrea replies, "You know I'm tired of this. Let's move it on. Here's the offer." Ted has gotten insight as to what the body language meant. He knows exactly why his opponent displayed this body language.

Ted decided to call Andrea's bluff: "I'll tell you what. I guess we're not going to come to an agreement." Ted stood up to leave the room. Looking at Ted standing in front of her, Andrea thought, "I need this deal more than Ted does, and I thought he was going to be an easy person." "Wait a minute, Ted. Come back, sit down. Ted smiled to himself as he recognized his change in body language moved Andrea from hard to possibly closed or open node. Ted began a process of asking for concessions and making offers.

The Dangers of Hard Nodes Clashing

I want you to envision a very combative deposition of an expert witness. Richard, the plaintiff attorney, and Kevin, the defense attorney, detest each other. The tension in the room is rising. They take every opportunity to verbally attack each other. At the end of the deposition Kevin goes out into the waiting room of Richard's law firm and says, "I don't feel like leaving your law firm. *Make me* leave your law firm. Go ahead, make me. Just make me get out of your law firm." Richard stares at him in bewilderment as Kevin edges closer to him.

Richard needs to understand how to handle the situation and why Kevin is taking this position. Richard might ask, "Did I do something to alienate you? Can you please give me more insight as far as why you're behaving this way?" Richard is thinking, "I dislike this guy and he is acting like a real hard nose." The scene in the waiting room, which is being observed by a client and the receptionist, is turning ugly. Kevin moves closer to Richard and reaches his arm out toward Richard's chest.

What caused this confrontation? How would you handle it? First, you need to understand the person's mind-set before you offer a solution to it. Here's what could have caused Kevin's reactions. Suppose Richard said something about the yellow suit Kevin had on and he took offense to it. If this happened, this was the starting point for the alienation that developed. Then Richard turned the heat in the room down when he sensed his opponent was getting overheated. Kevin noticed Richard doing this. That was the second factor in Kevin's antagonism.

The third aspect was that Richard's expert witness did an excellent job testifying; she did not cave in under Kevin's pressure. The combination of a perceived insult, uncomfortable environment, and frustration with the expert's testimony further pushed Kevin toward his irrational behavior. Kevin wanted to even the score, typical of hard types.

As a negotiator, you need to understand what caused your opponent to take a position. The sooner you address it, the better the chance to de-escalate a potentially dangerous situation. Adroit and rapid analysis helps you find the right solution to fix the right problem. You don't want to apply the wrong solution to the problem.

In this situation, Richard thought, "You want to be a hard-nose type? I can be too." He picked up the phone in his waiting room and dialed 911. He said, "There's a man in my law firm who will not leave. I would like to have an officer come to remove him from my building." With that, Kevin hit the down button on the elevator and disappeared.

Richard had several choices in terms of how to respond to Kevin's behavior. He could have walked away from the lobby to his own office. There was a risk Kevin might have followed him away from the open lobby area. Richard could have touched Kevin to show him where the elevator was, but likely Kevin would have hit him, something he was aching to do. Richard might have attempted to mollify Kevin if his anger had not made it impossible to reason or negotiate with him. Instead, Richard used a show of force by calling the police to encourage Kevin to leave. As Richard watched the elevator doors close, he thought "What a jerk! I wish I did not have to deal with him again."

What you do today influences tomorrow's negotiation situation. Kevin was forced to back down; Richard suspected Kevin would seek other ways to get even as the litigation progressed. Richard's heavy-handedness may not have been necessary as opposed to helping Kevin calm down. Given the ongoing relationship between these two attorneys, Richard may have harmed his future negotiation efforts. He thought he was winning the battle but he could have been losing the war. Always be cautious about how you address any situation. Never appear to be heavy-handed.

There were a couple of important events that followed the scene in the waiting room. In making inquiries, Richard learned that many attorneys suspected Kevin was mentally ill. Second, they carried their battle into the courtroom when Kevin made anti-Semitic comments about Richard in front of a judge. The local legal newspaper carried the story about how the incident escalated into an even more unpleasant confrontation on a personal level in the courtroom.

Think about how that could have been prevented if Richard had been able to defuse Kevin's anger. You're always negotiating. What you do today influences tomorrow's outcomes.

Looking for Commonalities

An astute negotiator watches body language signals to find common ground with an opponent. For example, you lean toward Felicity, your opponent. She leans toward you. "You and I are similar," this says. We're talking and sitting across from one another. I cross my right leg; Felicity crosses hers. I stand up; she stands up. That's a leading signal; it fosters a sense of being similar: "My opponent is just like me."

Tap the power of leading your opponent with your body language. Subliminally build rapport with body language and nonverbal signals by initially doing exactly what I recommended: the other negotiator crosses her right leg and you cross your right leg. The other negotiator happens to shift her position as she's seated. You shift your position.

So far you've been following the other negotiator's lead. All of a sudden, rub your eye. (Make sure you don't rub your eye at a time when your gesture could be interpreted as not believing what you are seeing.) The other negotiator rubs her eye also.

I'm being a little theatrical by suggesting rubbing your eye. The signals can be very subtle also. As an example, you slow the pace of your speech; she slows the pace of her speech. At that point you're leading her. You're building invisible rapport as the result of the nonverbal body language gestures that the two of you have mimicked. You mimicked her and now she mimicked you.

The point is to watch for who is doing the leading. You believe you are leading her. But it is only because Felicity is giving you the same signals you gave her to that you think you are leading her. Felicity wants you to believe that. As you go further into the negotiation, watch for shifts in the leading. When you uncross your legs, Felicity keeps hers crossed. Observe exactly when it occurred and what was said at the time. It may be a signal she's no longer following your lead.

Suppose Felicity uncrosses her legs several minutes later. Try crossing your legs again to see what she does. When she does not cross hers, this may confirm you are not leading her. There are all kinds of subtle signals you can send with your body language to determine to what degree you can lead the other negotiator. In so doing you get greater insight as to who is really in control of the negotiation.

Introducing Commonalities

I started the chapter with Toby and Clarise talking at the beginning of a meeting with what seemed like idle chatter. Toby asked probing questions of Clarise to bring out her education and her work experience. He focused on their common ground.

The timing of when to introduce commonalities depends on the personality nodes of the negotiators. Do that as soon as possible with the very easy, open and closed negotiator types to build the perception, "My opponent is just like me. I like this person." The affinity principle starts to become enhanced.

Be cautious with the hard negotiator type. Use a deeper, more forceful tone with that type. The deeper tone says, "I am an authority." How you pitch your voice either conveys or cedes authority. If you raise your voice at the end of a sentence you may sound tentative or timid.

The hard person may perceive you as a pushover if you attempt to quickly build rapport. Always be cautious about the timing of how you start to build the rapport process based on the node type you're negotiating with.

When Discretion Is the Better Part of Valor

Withhold your knowledge about commonalities instead of sharing them at the beginning of a negotiation when your opponent has had an embarrassing situation occur in his life and you've had a similar situation occur in yours. Don't build rapport off of something that would embarrass someone: "Oh, you went to prison? I went to prison too. You were at Sing Sing years ago? I was at Sing Sing years ago also." Don't invoke bad memories by referring to unpleasant experiences. In a business environment you would not want to build any type of rapport off of something that's uncomfortable.

In Summary

Identify your opponent's node by leading with your body language, tactics, and strategies: leaning forward, leaning back, crossing your leg, uncrossing your leg, smiling, and not smiling.

You will also know to what degree this person will follow you. Understand why people adopt the demeanor they are trying to project so you can get an insight into their thought processes.

Observe how the other negotiator's demeanor changes during your interaction. Be mindful of when a trigger causes the person to switch nodes. Is your opponent moving toward a more open or more closed position? He shuts down when he moves from open to closed. He becomes more receptive when he transitions from hard to closed; he's moving more progressively toward understanding and being more receptive to what's occurring in the negotiation. You've achieved steps in the path to success when you are able to move a closed or hard negotiator to a more open or easy position.

Chapter 8

✱ ✱ ✱ ✱ ✱ ✱ ✱ ✱ ✱ ✱ ✱ ✱

Persuaders: *Tapping the Power of Influence*

Carrie Townsend stood on the stage, about ready to make her presentation to a group of Internet marketers. After scanning the room and seeing a large space between the stage and the first row of seats, she stepped off the stage and said, "Bring your chairs forward and gather around." Carrie started her presentation with a story; she watched people lean toward her. After she skillfully slipped in content from the topic of her book, she asked, "Who would like a copy of this book?" Hands went up; she passed out the book to anyone who had a hand up. Carrie wove her net tighter by stressing the benefits and value of what she had to offer. "Who would like a free ticket to my next event? There are only 40 tickets and you will get them today, but when they are gone, they are gone." More hands went up.

When Carrie sensed she had created a sense of scarcity and urgency, she went into her sales pitch: a year-long coaching program with a lot of access to her. Clutching their free books and free tickets, a stream of people headed to the back of the room to sign up.

Negotiation strategies are much like what Carrie did to sell her services—they are rooted in the ability to persuade and influence others. This chapter focuses on some of the fundamentals of persuasion and influence that affect the negotiation process.

Win–Win or Win–Lose?

Does there always have to be a winner and a loser in a negotiation? Does your opponent think in terms of one winner and one loser in a negotiation? What kind of person are you negotiating with? This attitude may be rooted in negative negotiation experiences, cultural conditioning, or aggression. You may also encounter people who stubbornly refuse to allow you to lead, influence, or persuade them. When you're negotiating with someone and he accepts the premise of "I win, you lose," it's going to be very difficult to persuade him. You must show him that you're not a threat to him. And you might have to be a little more stringent with this type of individual simply because you need to let him know, "I'm willing to go toe-to-toe with you. We may have a difficult negotiation." Taking this stance should earn you respect, disarm the other negotiator, and help you move away from "I win, you lose" positioning. If that individual sees your negotiation style as similar to his, you are building on the affinity principle discussed in Chapter 7: people like us if they perceive we are like them. The likeability factor influences our ability to persuade others.

How do you spot the person who values cooperation and endorses a "win–win" position? This person values harmony and conflict avoidance. She says, "I'll go along to get along." With that type of individual, you can show through your actions that you're not out to harm her. Let her take the lead if that is appropriate. Allow her to feel comfortable with you. The more comfortable she becomes with you, the more she will intuitively trust you. This allows you to gently take the lead in the negotiation. You can do this through the questions that you ask. Test her reaction to see to what degree she will follow you. This negotiator allows you to persuade her because you've shown her that you're not going to harm her; you have a common goal of a win–win result.

Suppose you encounter a timid person who is overwhelmed by the negotiation and feels inadequate? This person may be afraid to follow you because he doesn't know if he can trust you. Show this person you can be trusted; allow him to take the lead. Use questions such as, "What do you think about this?" A smart negotiator would have set the scenario so the response the person gives is the one that harmoniously moves the negotiation forward. Build harmony by saying, "You're right. That's a good thought." Your response endorses the person's thought processes and helps him feel comfortable with you. He gains more courage when you accept his position; he feels as though he can trust you more, which allows you to persuade him.

Persuasion and Influence

Persuasion is the foundation of the ability to influence your opponents. If you cannot persuade them, you will not have influence over them. Your ability to influence others is a step toward persuading them; they have *allowed* you to take that first step in the form of persuasion. You gain influence to the degree that the other negotiators allow you to persuade them. Notice I said to the degree you're allowed to gain that form of persuasion necessary for influencing the other negotiators. All of us are in control of our lives. We don't relinquish control of our lives until we decide to literally give our power to someone else. That's how influence actually comes about. First you set the groundwork, whereby the other negotiators allow you to persuade them to trust you. Others watch you and judge whether you are attempting to help or harm their negotiation position. Always recognize your strategies are designed to gain influence over the other negotiators. You achieve this by

- teaching people a new way to think,
- challenging the way people currently think, and
- role modeling behaviors that will lead to a successful outcome.

The other negotiators have to allow you to use these strategies. You can be the smartest person in the world; you can be the sharpest negotiator in the world. You can outline the steps in the negotiation—show the negotiators the path that leads to a successful outcome for the negotiation. Yet if they refuse to cooperate, you have no persuasion over these individuals. You have no influence.

Consider this example: Krishnamurthy Iyengar learned how to negotiate by watching his mother talk to the fresh-vegetable vendors. His mother used a variety of strategies such as acting shocked at the price or starting to walk away when she did not hear an acceptable price. Through repeated experiences, he absorbed the lesson that one should never pay the first price that the vendor quoted. Krishnamurthy carried this belief into his negotiations when he started his electronics company. Ray Fox was puzzled when Krishnamurthy immediately rejected a price for parts Ray knew Krishnamurthy needed. Ray retreated, thought about Krishnamurthy's reaction, and consulted a partner who had encountered this strategy before. After taking over the negotiation, the partner started by quoting a price that was higher than the one he expected Krishnamurthy to accept. They concluded the negotiation at a price that was acceptable to them both and was very close to the price Ray initially quoted.

Sometimes it's not just necessarily the message that fails, it's the messenger. You may be the wrong messenger to deliver the message; someone else may be better able to connect with the other negotiator. If you are in such a situation, bring in your partner to negotiate.

Good Cop/Bad Cop

Made famous by police interviews with suspects, this technique typically uses two people. The bad cop is the person trying to deliver the message to the suspect that he or she should adopt a certain course of action, such as confessing to a crime. The good cop comes in to support and encourage the suspect. Often the good cop supplies food or beverages that the bad cop denied to the suspect. The good cop's behavior is designed to contrast with the bad cop's so the suspect will let his guard down. The bad cop is stern and harsh in an effort to make the suspect fearful. When good cop/bad cop is used during a negotiation, this technique is particularly devastating to the timid negotiator, who may retreat.

The person who has the "I win, you lose" perspective may go toe-to-toe with a person displaying the characteristics of the bad cop simply because he's going to show the bad cop exactly how tough he can be. When you bring in the good cop approach, you've already softened that individual, who may think to himself, "I'm tired of going through this whole game." A good negotiator will recognize the good cop/bad cop scenario even when it's projected by the same person. These nuances have an impact on the level of influence or persuasion one will have in a negotiation.

You can incorporate good cop/bad cop strategies in your negotiation without having two people present. Consider this example: Richard Allen was a businessman who saw the opportunity to make a lot of money by being part of the games development industry. He approached a programmer, Kevin Weinstein, to develop a new game. The contract included language that was very restrictive of the programmer's rights to his own intellectual property that had nothing to do with the new game. When Kevin confronted him with the offensive clauses, Richard said, "That's just boilerplate language. You know how lawyers are."

Recognizing good cop/bad cop, Kevin immediately had to make a decision about retaining an attorney to represent his interests against the "bad cop/lawyer" who created the contract. After deciding to see if he could revise the contract without an attorney, Kevin removed the parts of the contract that he believed were detrimental to his rights. He emphasized the value of his contribution to the game development by outlining all of the roles he was capable of playing. Then Kevin said to Richard, "What are you trying to do to me? You're trying to restrict me from working for any other game developer, and to take my intellectual property from me. I don't think so. That's not going to happen at all. The language in the contract is insulting." After expressing his displeasure with Richard's terms, Kevin found that Richard quickly agreed with Kevin's changes. He also agreed to an hourly rate that was three times higher than Kevin's current rate, and he offered a small percentage ownership in the company.

Kevin's negotiation incorporated several negotiation strategies. Richard most likely capitulated because Kevin recognized he had the power in the negotiation. Richard had no backup plan if Kevin pulled out of the project. Power equaled influence. Kevin had to choose to what degree he would allow Richard to influence him. Had he not said anything, the language in the contract would have bound Kevin to unfavorable terms. Influence is critical in a negotiation. Kevin recognized how his power influenced the negotiation.

Positional power is power that one gains in a negotiation as the result of being at a particular point in the negotiation and having something your opponent really wants. Kevin used his positional power to negotiate a higher hourly rate and obtain partial ownership of the company. He understood how to use his power to revise the agreement to make it acceptable to Richard and himself.

Influential Strategies

How do we gain influence over people? Consider the idea that you gain influence when you teach others a new way to think. This goes beyond what instructors or professors do within a higher educational setting. Certainly they challenge others to think differently. A good negotiator also challenges the other negotiator to consider different approaches to reach a successful outcome.

I coach people literally around the world on how they not only can reach a high level of performance, but consistently sustain that high level of performance on a daily basis. The individuals who I coach have already acknowledged my expertise. They've given me the right to have influence over them. I have positional power at that particular point. They know that what I possess will be of benefit to them; they allow me to influence them because that's why they are seeking my help. The people I coach want me to do just that—to influence them into performing better and achieving more in their lives.

We can only gain influence when someone allows us to. We lose influence once that person has been satisfied with the fact that she's received as much benefit as possible. When that happens, when we start to lose influence, we can use strategies to draw the person back to us. We can either point out a shortcoming, or offer more services. Compare this to the sales process you may be familiar with: You may have seen marketers who offer a variety of upsells by saying, "Oh but wait, there's more." Once again you turn to look at the commercial or whatever has drawn your attention back to it.

Use the same type of tactic in a negotiation. You might say something like, "If you like what I've already told you, let me tell you what else you need to know." This strategy is used to influence the other negotiator to help you both reach the goal of the negotiation. Your influence ends when the person pushes back, and says, "I'm good. I don't need anymore." In a negotiation, that's the number-one reason you need to exercise your influence while it lasts. Once we lose influence we lose the ability to persuade others to move in a particular direction.

Body Language and Influence

Chapter 1 discusses the crucial importance of being able to read the subtle and not so subtle signals of body language. Let's suppose you see the other negotiator resisting your attempts to influence him. What can you do when that happens? As you will see, there are several different actions you can take. First of all, before you ever get to the negotiation table, you need to understand the style of the person with whom you'll be negotiating:

- What motivates that person?
- Why he is negotiating with you?
- What is he going to do if he can't actually achieve the goals that he's seeking?

Consider this situation: Vincent Berelli was negotiating with Sara Harter, the head of procurement for a major pharmaceutical client. He observed Sara's body language and gestures as he sincerely said, "I'm going to give you the best deal that I can. I'm going to make sure you're happy with it." Vincent knew that Sara was motivated to save money for her company. She was under pressure to reduce costs. But he saw Sara lean back in her chair. Vincent perceived Sara as literally moving away from his words. "Doesn't she trust me?" he wondered. Vincent asked, "Do you believe what I'm saying?" Sara leaned back further and replied, "Yes, I do." Vincent recognized this mixed message. Sara said, "Yes," but her body language said "No."

Skillfully reading Sara's body language, Vincent said, "I heard what you said." He *meant*, "I heard exactly what you said, but I saw you lean away from me. That gesture suggests that maybe you don't really believe me. Convince me that you believe me." Sara leaned toward him, smiled, and said, "I was a little apprehensive, but let's go on and see what happens."

Vincent recognized from Sara's body language that she was skeptical, but he did not disclose his thoughts. Instead, he gently challenged her. Her body language of leaning forward indicated that she was at least willing to listen openly. Vincent rejoiced at the possibility that he could have some influence over Sara; he knew he had to conclude a successful negotiation that afternoon. His supervisor had stressed the importance of Sara's business.

Vincent watched Sara's body language as he proceeded through the negotiation: Sara continued to lean away from him, frown, and keep her arms crossed over her chest. "I'm not getting anywhere," he thought. "I need to regroup and back out of this negotiation."

Don't invest more of your time in the negotiation when you recognize from the other person's body language and responses that you are not gaining influence. You think, "But I've spent so much time on this. I want to see it to the end." The more time you invest in a negotiation, the more you are apt to allow yourself to be drawn deeper into the negotiation. This puts you at risk for making concessions that jeopardize your position. When you see this temptation arising, back out of the negotiation. Depending on the situation, consider bringing in another stronger negotiator. This person might be your supervisor, or someone the other person may respect or might be able to relate to more easily. Understand the dynamics and body language when it comes to influence and act accordingly.

Something as important as sitting or standing during a negotiation can affect influence. Suppose one person stands while the other remains seated. How does this relate to influence? Ask yourself, "Does the person who is standing perceive herself as being in a superior position? Is she saying, "I'm bigger and more powerful?" The person who is standing will usually have the control. When you see your opponent standing, you should consider standing up also to neutralize the other person's attempt to gain influence.

But let's look at this body language from another point of view. Suppose the other person has a higher level of power. Think of a king sitting on a throne. In children's books, the king is never shown as *standing* in front of his throne. He stays seated while his subjects come to him.

Let's look at another situation about how sitting or standing is used to convey power and influence. Consider this scenario: Ellen Dewar was sitting behind her desk when George Alwick entered her office. They were both vice presidents of the same company. Ellen remained seated when George came up to her desk and shook her hand. George flared with resentment. He thought, "She thinks she is so important that she does not have to stand up while I shake her hand. That is really impolite." If Ellen had stood up to shake George's hand, she would be acknowledging through that action that she and George were equals. Ellen has already sent a message, intended or not, that set the tone for the negotiation.

Along with some colleagues, I had the opportunity to meet a U.S. senator in Washington, D.C. The senator sat in a chair as we were filing past him to shake his hand. I responded to what I believed his body language was saying: he felt he was a prestigious U.S. senator. I perceived him thinking, "Yes, lowly ones, you come by, shake my hand and if you're really fortunate I'll let you kiss my ring." Believing that was what he was trying to project, I thought to myself, "Okay, Mr. Important, I'm going to see how long you sit in this chair when I shake your hand." I shook his hand so hard he grimaced and stood up because of the pain I created. I said, "Oh, Mr. Senator, I'm sorry" in a cynical voice.

Consider the strategies you might use when the other negotiator is sitting and you are standing, such as changing the loudness of your voice. Speak slower or softer so the other person has to lean in or stand to hear you. And if you really want to drive the point home, you can literally start to get down to his level—you could bend or kneel down. Getting onto your knees should stimulate the other person to look for a way so that you could both sit or both stand. If the person was not deliberately trying to assume a position of power, you may receive an apology for putting you through the discomfort.

Subliminal Messages and Influence

As noted in Chapter 5, *subliminal* persuasion has a role in negotiation. Here's an example of the use of subliminal messaging to influence others. Roberto Gomez was a graphic artist for a major publisher. Deborah Samuels worked with Roberto as the editor. The day before the first production meeting about the book, Deborah said, "Roberto, this is what the book is about." As she described the book, Roberto leaned back, closed his eyes, and developed a strong sense of what color should be used for the cover. At the production meeting, he displayed his preference for the color of the book cover by wearing a tie that matched the color. Deborah observed the way Roberto sent subliminal messages through his choice of ties. "He wants a mauve cover for that book," she realized. "I'm not so sure that is a good idea."

When Roberto realized Deborah expected him to advocate for a color through his choice of a tie, he decided to exert his influence by switching his strategy. At the next production meeting, he wore a pink tie. Even though the two colors were closely aligned with one another, Deborah thought, "That's ugly. I would never publish a book cover that's pink. Let's go with mauve." Roberto knew he had achieved his goal of subliminally influencing Deborah by picking the pink color he knew she would hate and would drive her to his first choice of mauve.

This tactic is also called "reverse psychology"—sending a message that is opposite to what you want the person to do. Think of the parent who tells her teenager: "No, you don't have to do your homework today. No, it's not important, but if you do want to use the car . . . ." There's also a subliminal message: "If one day you want to be able to buy a car as nice as this you may think about doing your homework today, tomorrow, and the next day. You will be able to afford a car like this by getting a better education."

Overt Persuasion

Overt persuasion is the opposite of subliminal messages. Leaning forward or backward, frowning, sitting, or standing are overt aspects of body language. You may use overt persuasion in the choice of your words. Consider a negotiating situation in which the other negotiator is your employee who wants to achieve more in her life. For example, you are discussing an opening in the department that would represent a move up for your employee. She wants to get that position so she can earn more money and prestige. You want to motivate her to make changes within the department so that she would be eligible for a promotion. You might say, "Here's what will occur if you receive this promotion, and this is what you need to do to be considered." You point out exactly what her goals are for the negotiation. You are overtly telling her if she follows this particular path that this will be the outcome that she will receive. She allows you to persuade and gain influence over her.

There are benefits of combining both overt and subliminal persuasion. For example, you note the other negotiator is skeptical about your intentions. He says, "I believe what you're saying," but you hear doubt in his voice. You respond to the subliminal message underlying the overt message by asking, "What is it that you're hesitant about?" "Oh, I'm not hesitant," he replies. What he has shown to you is that he doesn't want to be perceived as hesitant. What does that mean from a negotiation point of view? You are aware he is hesitant but doesn't want to be viewed as such, so you proceed keeping in mind his words and tone are in conflict.

Be careful of how you use overt and subliminal persuasion in a negotiation. Don't allow one dimension to overwhelm the other. Both types of messages give you information about the other negotiator. When you send overt and subliminal messages, they should be congruent. Otherwise, you may be perceived as being dishonest. You may lose the influence and then you will definitely lose the ability to persuade.

Power strategies directly relate to your degree of influence. Power is fluid. You have it one moment; you don't the next.

Strategies you use when you have less power will result in different outcomes simply because the balance of power shifted. You risk further losses of your influence and persuasion ability. Your goal changes to regaining your power.

Social Proof and Influence

Marie Rivera walked into April Johnson's office with the goal of negotiating a fee to become a sales consultant for April's company. April said, "How do I know you are any good? Who else have you worked with?" Maria pulled out a stack of letters she received from satisfied clients, some were large, well-known companies. After April scanned the first few letters, she put them aside, and said, "Now, let's talk."

Social proof is used both before and during negotiation. It involves you gathering or referring to testimonials from satisfied clients in order to bolster credibility or increase your expert status. The people with whom you are negotiating have a need for safety and reassurance. Capitalize on this need. Point to a situation when you helped another client *like them* obtain a positive outcome. Social proof can reduce the anxiety of the other person with whom you're negotiating.

Today's savvy negotiator shares social proof through company websites, brochures, flyers, other marketing material, and social media. Past abuses involving the use of testimonials led to regulations to prevent fraudulent use of social proof. The most convincing social proof shares these characteristics:

- They are real comments by real people. The comments can be verified with written documentation.
- They are in video form. Video testimonials from well-known or respected people are the most credible.

- They include a photo of the person, if they are not in video form.
- The name, position, and location of the person are included: "Bill Walters, CEO of Wonderful Inc., New York, New York," rather than "Bill W. from New York."
- They are specific about some aspect of your services, rather than general comments like "Jan is terrific."
- They include a measurable outcome that occurred as the result of working with you (such as "We saved our company $500,000 as the result of the negotiation strategies we learned from Greg Williams.").
- The testimonials relate to the services you are offering to the client and are of comparable value. For example, if you are negotiating for a half-million-dollar contract, your testimonials should relate to other similar-size deals.

Optics and Influence

Optics encompass visual aspects of our behavior. How do you display that behavior? You walk into a negotiation in well-fitting clothes, like you are the proudest and most confident person in the world. You drive a fine car and live in a fine house. The other negotiator observes you and your behavior; your goal is that you are seen as credible. On the other hand, you may choose to downplay an air of success. For example, if you don't want to pay more for a service than you have to, don't walk into that situation projecting an air of wealth.

Optics play an important role in a negotiation. Consider this scenario: Salesmen avoided approaching a plainly dressed woman who walked into a furniture store. They reached conclusions about her based on her optics—her clothes, age, and race—and did not approach her. After she wandered around the store looking for help, one of the salesman decided to talk to her. To his delight, she bought furniture to fill an entire house, and paid for her purchase with the highest level of American Express credit card. The salesman who received a commission on her sale was thrilled he took the initiative to wait on her. His coworkers learned an important lesson about relying too heavily on optics.

I encountered a similar situation of not getting appropriate attention when I went into a Mercedes dealership to buy a new car. Spotting my casual clothing, the salesman who came up to me treated me as though I was there to kick the tires and basically dismissed me. I thought, "How dare you?" After I bought a new car from another dealership, I went back to the original dealership a few days later, asked to speak to the manager, and told him exactly what had occurred. The manager said, "We've gotten a lot of complaints about this individual. He's no longer with us." They had gotten rid of that person. This salesman dismissed me based on the optics—he concluded I did not have the money to purchase a car and thus he did not want to waste his time. The same thing may happen in a negotiation. Good negotiators know how to use optics to benefit their position and will do so.

Don't be dismissive just because the optics appear to be out of alignment with the person's mannerisms and ability to deliver.

Scarcity and Urgency

"Hurry now, there's only five left and four people are on the line right now trying to grab them." That's scarcity used in a sales context. The concept of scarcity is most often encountered in sales situations and can be effectively used in a negotiation. A negotiator might use scarcity to apply pressure on the other person by saying there are only so many of whatever it is that you might be negotiating for: "Get it while you can get it. This is a rare find. Only a few of these exist." Scarcity is used to increase a price or to stimulate a buying decision.

"The offer expires at midnight. Buy now." That's *urgency* woven into a sales pitch. Negotiators use urgency to press for a decision while the other negotiator would prefer to think it over and not make a commitment right at the moment.

There are risks associated with using scarcity and urgency. A savvy negotiator may call your bluff. Consider this scenario: Denny Sharmal sold beach equipment. He had 100 beach chairs in his storage room. He knew the season was changing and he needed to get rid of those chairs as fast as possible. Kara Knightly bought beach equipment at the end of the season. Denny decided to apply the influence factors of scarcity and urgency, and told her, "There are only a few left" (scarcity). "You better get them while they're here and while they last" (urgency). Kara responded, "Okay, I'll get back to you."

Denny's lie trapped himself in a corner from a negotiation perspective. When Kara returned a week later, Denny still had 100 beach chairs; he could not offload them to another buyer. What did Denny's actions tell Kara? She now knew Denny used scarcity and urgencies as ploys. She thought, "I have all the power in this situation and Denny knows it. Denny is asking $10 for each chair but I know I can get them for $4. She called his bluff by offering $4 a piece. Denny learned the lesson and became cautious about how he used scarcity and urgency in his next negotiation. Be very cautious as to how you use scarcity and urgency in a negotiation because it can backfire on you.

My motto is, "You are always negotiating." The strategies you use today set the stage for actions you will take in the future. Kara will remember that Denny was not truthful with her. She will not give Denny the level of influence he needs to negotiate with her in the future.

Social proof, scarcity, and urgency may be combined to conclude a negotiation. A coach might say, "I can only take on so many clients. I would like you to be one of them, but once I am at full capacity, I will need to create a waiting list and I can't guarantee I will have space for you." Consider this situation: Jessica Holmes offered a business coaching program; Laura Brasher was interested in the program. She knew she needed help, but she was hesitant to join. Sensing Laura's indecision, Jessica explained, "I am enrolling people into the program at the rate of one or two a month. I currently have 12 people in the program and will cap it at 15. Laura, if you want to get the benefits of this program, now is the time to commit." Jessica's approach incorporates scarcity, urgency, and social proof. "Other people are joining the program" provided the social proof.

Jessica probed to find out what was preventing Laura from enrolling in the program. "You've expressed an interest in joining the program. You can see that others are coming into the program. What's holding you back?" Laura responded, "I'm still not ready to come into the program." Jessica inquired, "Just out of curiosity, so I could better know how to serve you, what's the real reason that you don't want to come into the program?" Laura replied, "I am taking on a partner in a few months and I am concerned about the expenses." Jessica said, "If you became part of this coaching program we could work together to properly structure the business to absorb this new person. With my help, we can discuss her role and compensation. Perhaps you would be better off starting her as a subcontractor. We would discuss whether a partnership is the right role for her."

Next, Laura said, "I know your help would be invaluable, but I am not ready to commit to the program. Could I have you on speed dial and call you whenever I have a problem?" Jessica gently rebuffed Laura's attempt to negotiate a new service that Jessica was not prepared to supply. She knew that Laura might not become a coaching client then, but that Jessica's expertise and positional power was strong enough that when Laura was ready for assistance, she would return.

In Summary

Your ability to influence your opponent is made up of a mix of factors:

- your persuasiveness in introducing a new factor into the negotiation that sways her perspective,
- your beliefs about whether the negotiation is a win–win or win–lose situation and her perspective of the same,
- your body language, overt and subliminal messages, and
- careful use of scarcity and urgency.

When you have established your ability to influence the other person, you have a greater opportunity to reach an outcome that will satisfactorily conclude the negotiation.

Chapter 9

✦ ✦ ✦ ✦ ✦ ✦ ✦ ✦ ✦ ✦ ✦ ✦

Techniques: *Creating a Successful Negotiation*

Plaintiff attorney Walter Garrett stared across the room at defense attorney Sarah Jenner. Walter's client Jessica Davis had suffered neck and back injuries, fractured ribs, and a head injury. After months of treatment, Jessica had chronic pain. Her brain injury prevented her from being able to return to her job as an accountant. Jessica's debts were mounting. Her landlord had given her an eviction notice. "Please settle my case for as much as you can," she told Walter. "I am reaching the end of my rope."

Sarah said, "I know you want $750,000 for your client. Frankly, I don't agree your client's case is worth that. My carrier is prepared to offer $350,000." "Outrageous," sputtered Walter. "My client has a lost wages claim of $300,000 alone."

Sarah replied, "I may be able to get the carrier to agree to $550,000. How about we split the difference?"

Consider the tactics the attorneys used to negotiate Jessica's settlement. Sarah's offer to split the difference revealed how far she was willing to go to settle the claim. As she spoke, Walter noted her body language: her nonverbal gestures, tone, and the earnestness of her speech. If someone conveys sentiments in a half-hearted manner, she will be perceived in a half-hearted manner. From a negotiation point of view, you always have to be aware of not only the counteroffers you make, but the way in which you position your offers based on your demeanor.

Cracking the Wall

Have you ever wished you could get your opponent to disclose his strategy? Here is what to look for. Watch the other negotiator's body language and demeanor, which is particularly important when you suspect the other negotiator is not being as open as he should be. You can deliberately provoke a reaction by using your body language to convey suspicion. Lean away from the other negotiator as he's talking. Look him directly in the eye to see if he avoids your stare.

Observe for clusters of body language, such as him leaning back while crossing his arms, looking away from you, and avoiding eye contact altogether. Consider the clusters related to the offers and counteroffers being discussed.

Picture yourself as a real estate agent who is sitting with a man, Len Friedman, who wants to purchase a house. Mario Vincenti is the seller, who is sitting across from him. You observe Mario leaning away from your buyer. When Len makes an offer, all of a sudden not only does Mario start to lean toward Len, but he smiles. His hands are open with palms up. He's indicating through that gesture that he is more open not only to the offer that Len has made but he may also be willing to follow Len's lead. As the man's Realtor, you should be very aware of the body language signals so you can get glimpses of thought processes and guide your client.

Using Statistics to Make a Point

People are fond of quoting statistics to bolster their opinion or to support an argument. How effective is this strategy in a negotiation? The answer is mixed. The usefulness of quoting statistics is based on the type of individual with whom you are negotiating. Some folks love data and numbers. Others find their eyes glazing over under a barrage of numbers.

Use your body language to emphasize a particular statistic, which is even more useful if you think the other person is not astute enough to see the significance of the statistic you're using. As an example, you are a public speaker who is meeting with a potential client to discuss booking your services to work with the sales team of a large corporation. You lean toward the other person and say, "I'm 100% sure based on what I've experienced this is the best action for you to take." Let's say your body language is aligned with that pronouncement even to the point that you're either using a finger to point to your opponent or stabbing your finger toward the table. You're emphasizing the fact that the statistic that you are quoting from your perspective is valid.

If you are toward the end of a negotiation, and find a slight impasse, you may wish to use statistics to emphasize the fact that the other negotiator should not be alarmed by following the course that you've suggested. You can say something like, "75% of the companies who have brought me in to train their sales team have seen average increases in revenues of 25% per year."

If you observe your opponent's body language as being somewhat skeptical, you can then refer to the social proof or testimonials you received from companies that experienced those improvements. Literally show her the outcome of what you cited. That will carry even more emphasis and becomes a nonverbal gesture that you interject into the negotiation, which allows you to be perceived as more persuasive. During the discussions, use gestures to point to the testimonials whenever you want to emphasize your credibility and reiterate the statistics of success.

Pain and Pleasure in a Negotiation

Preliminary research prior to a negotiation helps you understand what will motivate the other negotiators. Missy and Charles Chadwick sat in front of Jose, a car salesman. Missy was pain adverse. She wanted to conclude the deal that day. She was very tired of driving her 10-year-old car and couldn't wait to finish this deal so she could look forward to having a safe, new car. She was not willing to wait for another day or another dealer to delay closing the deal. Missy was more easily swayed during a negotiation because of her motivation to avoid the pain of not coming up with a decisive conclusion to the negotiation.

Jose observed the body language of Missy as she fumed over the protracted negotiations. She sighed, squirmed in her seat, and looked impatient. Jose also noted that Charles had been oblivious to his wife's signals. Charles was more willing to take risks and incur the pain of not concluding the purchase. Charles thought, "Okay, so if we don't buy this car today, I know I still have tomorrow. If it doesn't get done tomorrow, I know there are other car dealers in the area."

Sensing Charles's thought processes, Missy pulled him out in the hall away from the salesman and revealed the pain the protracted negotiations was causing her. Charles quickly capitulated after calculating the pain of not agreeing with his wife. Jose smiled when the couple returned ready to conclude the deal.

The pain and pleasure aspect enters a negotiation from a physical perspective when you literally turn up or decrease the heat in a room to make someone uncomfortable. You are forcing your opponent to experience a form of discomfort that can be somewhat aligned with pain. Your actions force the person to consider how long she wants to stay in an uncomfortable environment; that influences the length of the negotiation. This is another reason that you should consider who will be negotiating with you when you have a team. You want to be sure your team members do not fall prey to these tactics.

Now let's look at the pleasure aspect. There may be all kinds of additional goodies that you can put on the negotiation table, including food and beverages, that send a subliminal message of hospitality. You may also use promises of pleasure if the negotiation is satisfactorily concluded, such as extra bonuses. The goodies can also be held back to cause discomfort. You are sending a subliminal message that says, "If you do what I suggest it will be pleasurable for you because I'll make this negotiation easier. If you don't, it will be painful."

Exaggerated Pain or Pleasure Responses

Be wary of individuals who exaggerate their reactions during a negotiation. Jason helped corporations to improve their performance through executive coaching. Jason approached Geoffrey about purchasing his website development services. In the middle of the tense negotiation, Jason told Geoffrey, "Get your foot off my neck!" Although he was speaking metaphorically, he meant, "You are literally causing me pain with your offer." He communicated that he was in a painful situation based on Geoffrey's offer.

Geoffrey responded by being somewhat flip to lighten up the environment and alleviate the pain that Jason injected into the negotiation. Geoffrey said to himself, "Jason is trying to invoke pain and express displeasure simply as a ploy in a negotiation. He knows my offer of $300,000 is fairly priced. I will counter with a lower number."

Not happy with Geoffrey's counteroffer of $200,000, Jason replied, "Please, you're hurting me." He grabbed his heart as he leaned backwards, indicating that the negotiation was painful. His body language showed that he was struck with pain and tried to convince Geoffrey that he did not like the offer on the table.

Suppose Jason grabbed his heart and instead of leaning back, leaned toward Geoffrey while saying, "Oh, this is so painful for me." Geoffrey thought, "He is not sincere about the discomfort that he is in simply because he's leaning toward me. I'm going to test him and watch what he does next."

"I can't pay you any more than $220,000." Geoffrey watched Jason carefully as he opened his hands, saying "This is painful." His hands meant he was lowering his guard and being sincere with this gesture. They concluded the negotiation by agreeing to a price of $250,000.

What would you do? Knowing that Jason was using a ploy, Geoffrey could have held firm on his offer to get Jason to make the next move. Geoffrey could have enhanced the process by saying, "What would it take to relieve the pressure on your neck?" Jason might have given an offer that was higher than $250,000. When Geoffrey lowered his offer before asking Jason what might be fair to Jason, he left potential money on the table. Seek input from the other negotiator to gain insight into what he thinks is fair before lowering an offer. By getting his input, you know how your offer should be modified.

Exaggerated pleasure responses also give clues in a negotiation. Watch for smiles, a lilt in the voice, euphoric expressions, and other signs of happiness. Smiling is often accompanied by the person's voice going up. The other negotiator could be literally sitting taller in a chair across from you if you're negotiating face-to-face. That too gives you a signal along with the other cluster signals of the smile and the uplifting of the corners of the eyes.

Posture also conveys messages. Suppose you are standing in front of a negotiator. You notice she has her hands open and her arms away from her body. What she is saying is, "I have nothing to fear from you." All of those clustered signals are aligned with the person being happier. Those are just a few of the body language signals that you can observe to detect if someone is really in a pleasurable state of mind. When you're negotiating observe the body language signals that can also give insight into what degree someone is experiencing pain, pleasure, happiness, sadness, and so on.

Scents during Negotiations

You may use scents to create an unpleasant or pleasant environment. For example, infusers may pump scents into the air that may affect your negotiations. One way to evoke a sense of pain is to put people in an environment that doesn't have pleasant smells. You might be indicating that they should hurry up and get the deal done to get out of the environment. I've known negotiators who will bite a clove of garlic and then get close to the other negotiator to make him back off. The aggressive subliminal message that's being sent is, "Look, get this over with. You don't want to be so close to me because it may be detrimental to you." There's a subliminal message being sent with the garlic.

You may notice that deodorant has failed in the middle of the negotiation. The nonverbal body language of body odor could have several meanings. It could convey, "You're making me sweat so badly that my body odor is starting to take over. I'm alarmed and scared. This is so important to me."

You might take an aggressive position by drawing attention to your opponent's body odor.

You: "Wow, John, what happened?"

John: "What do you mean what happened?"

You: "Is this negotiation really getting tough for you?"

John: "Why do you ask that?"

You: "Well, it appears that you didn't even take time to bathe."

John: "Oh."

Watch John's body language. Does John literally sniff his underarms, which could be a clue that subliminally he was unaware of his odor? He says, "Yes, I guess I am focusing so much on this negotiation that I'm not taking time to take care of myself." Does your comment make John angry and intensify his reluctance to agree to terms favorable to you? John's demeanor after you inform him of his odor will give you insight into his mind-set. He might say, "OK, so the negotiation is getting to me, now what?" On the other hand, suppose John says, "Wow, I'm sorry; maybe we should convene at another time." You know that the negotiation is really affecting him; he's aware that you realize this, and he wants to put himself into a better light and smell.

Pleasant smells may enhance negotiations. Suppose you are going to negotiate with Grant to buy your bakery. You know he loves baking. You pick a back room in your bakery for the negotiations, and ask your staff to bake cookies while you are talking with Grant. As the air fills with the smell of cookies, you watch Grant smile as he subliminally starts to feel good about the environment. He transfers his good feelings to the negotiation.

Smells impact the senses and enhance what you wish to accomplish. From a body language point, you should observe what type of effects that scent is having on the other negotiator. Note whether or not she's smiling more as a result of the scent that has now been infused into the negotiation.

Skilled negotiators may be aware of the deliberate use of scents: "Wait a minute, this smells like a pine scent, which makes me think of Christmas time and Christmas trees. This is a ploy I'm going to ignore." While they may deliberately ignore that particular scent, they may also recognize how you are trying to influence their thought process and therefore raise their guard.

Detecting Lying

Sandra Edsoren watched Howard Weston as he responded to her offer of a job as director of Human Relations. She named the salary that she was prepared to offer. "I'm not really sure I want that responsibility now," he said. "He's lying," she thought. What gave him away? Before this discussion began, Sandra had studied Howard's eye movements and knew how he typically moved his eyes. (Refer back to Chapter 1 for the discussion on the meaning of eye movements.) Sandra watched his eyes as he spoke. She noted Howard would not look her in the eye and concluded he not only did not believe what he was saying, but that he was also somewhat ashamed and embarrassed. He did not want her to detect his lie by seeing it in his eyes.

Sandra thought, "I don't really believe what he is saying. What is he after? Does he want me to beg him to take the job? Is he angling for a higher salary than I offered?" Sandra replied, "What makes you think that?" As Howard responded, Sandra watched his body language. Howard continued to look away from her as he said, "I don't know if I have the skills to handle the job. But if I were to take it, I would need a considerably higher salary."

Note that Sandra did not confront Howard with his lie, but let him reveal his true motivation for hesitating.

Suppose instead, Sandra said to Howard, "I don't think you are being truthful with me by saying you are not ready for the responsibility." Howard sighed deeply and said, "I don't know why you would say I was lying. I don't know why you would challenge me." This display of wounded ego deepened Sandra's suspicion that Howard was looking for stroking. He wanted her to convince him that he has the skills to manage the department, and that Sandra really needed him in that position. Sandra knew she had to delve deeper into the source of his lie. The risk of not calling him on the lie would mean Sandra could be manipulated into giving a higher salary, when what Howard really wanted was ego stroking.

Howard would continue to lie if he thought he was getting away with it. He did not see what he was doing as lying. Stretching the truth was nothing more than his perception of a valid negotiation strategy. Sandra knew that if she allowed Howard to continue his positioning without being challenged, she would be giving Howard permission to lie to her. While Sandra felt by not challenging Howard she was giving him permission to lie, she could also be gathering additional insight that could prove to be more beneficial as the negotiation progressed.

As stated above, by not challenging Howard initially, Sandra was able to get Howard to disclose the real cause of him being less than completely truthful. He wanted more money! There'll be times when you will have to decide what time is appropriate to call someone on dishonesty. Before doing so, make sure that you've gathered the proper amount of insight to determine where you'll take the negotiation once you present your observation.

Trust strengthens a negotiation. Lying poisons it. Your guard goes up when you believe someone is lying to you. If you're the person who is being perceived as lying, the other negotiator may not believe the truth. She will start to question everything that you say; lies can poison and destroy the trust and honesty needed between negotiators. Lies can result in a misdirection of the negotiation that may lead to an impasse. A person who is lying experiences some form of discomfort. One lie may cause a slight bit of discomfort, while a barrage of lies will definitely create a level of discomfort that becomes easier to discern. Nevertheless, even at the outset of the first lie, the body will make a soothing gesture to correct for the untruthfulness. Be attuned to that soothing gesture, which could be in the form of someone's hand rubbing the opposite arm, leg, neck, hand, and so on. That soothing gesture will alert you to observe for gestures that will indicate the severity of the lies being told.

Dealing with Differing Perceptions

Suppose you're dealing with a person who has a different perception of the deal. How can you tell that individual is looking at this negotiation in a way that's really markedly different from your perspective? Start off the negotiation by discussing the outcome that both of you are seeking. This strategy helps to obtain the other person's buy-in and sets the stage for the outcome. As you are engaged in the negotiation you can reconfirm what the other negotiator is looking for, what you're looking for and what the two of you are negotiating for. When you get toward the conclusion of the negotiation you can then cite where it is that you were, where it is that you are, and where it is that you hope to be in a short period of time. This dialogue sounds something like this:

Mary: "Joe, we've come together to discuss how your organization can provide us with the planks we need in our manufacturing operations. As of now, your organization will provide us with 1,000 planks delivered on a weekly basis, correct?"

Joe: "Yes, Mary, that's correct. We'll do so and your organization will have a check to my company by the following Wednesday after delivery, correct?"

Mary: "Yes, that's correct. We'll also have a three-day grace period to make sure the mail doesn't negatively impact the arrival of the check and our agreement."

Joe: "That was not part of our discussion."

Mary: "You're right, but after thinking about the impact the mail might have on our agreement, I wanted to prevent such from occurring."

Joe: "That puts our agreement in a different light."

Mary: "How so?"

Joe: "We're depending on your check arriving by the following Wednesday after delivery, so our cash flow is not impacted."

Mary: "What other course of action might you suggest to make sure the mail doesn't negatively impact you receiving the check?"

Joe: "Can you wire the funds to our bank once you receive the shipment within a day?"

Mary: "Yes, we can do that."

Joe: "Thank you, Mary. It's really nice doing business with you."

Detect differing perceptions by observing the body language of the other negotiator. Does she speak quickly with a rising inflection in her voice? You've just confirmed she is excited. As an example, she says something along the lines of, "Wow, I really like the way that you and I are concluding this negotiation." You can tell from the excitement in her voice and her smiles that she is happy.

Suppose she says, "You know, I had a different perspective of what this negotiation was going to be about and what it is that we were negotiating for." She frowns, shakes her head, and says these words slowly. You've gotten a very different message.

A smart negotiation strategy would be to stop and inquire about her perspective to make sure the two of you are aligned or to at least confirm she is not using that as a ploy. Suspect a ploy if she said, "I had a different perspective" with a light voice while nodding her head. Those incongruent signals then indicate that it might be a ploy. Observe her body language after she said that. Here is a sample dialogue:

You: "But I thought you wanted the deal to be concluded by the end of this week."

Her: "Well, I do."

You: "If I gave you that, would you be agreeable to the price I quoted?"

Her: "Possibly."

Listen to her voice. If her voice rises as she says "possibly," she is responding more positively than if her voice goes down. The two intonations are slightly different. A falling inflection could mean "maybe I will or maybe I won't."

Group Negotiations

Up to this point in the chapter I've talked about negotiating against another person, but you could be involved in a negotiation with multiple people. The other side could have three or four people across the table and you might have a partner sitting next to you. Adding additional people to the negotiation setting provides an opportunity for differing perceptions to affect the negotiation.

There are times when the power person in a negotiation will not even be at the table. In some cases, depending on the magnitude of the negotiation, the person with the decision-making authority is not in the room. You may not know who that person is and with whom you're truly negotiating.

Let's say the power person is at the negotiation table. There are four people on the opposing side; you have three people on our side. You have to be much more cognizant of everyone's body language on the opposing team when you're negotiating with multiple negotiators. Some organizations will use a team of negotiators who have different roles in the negotiation. You will understand what those roles are from the body language, by observing who speaks at a particular time, what they speak about, who glances at others, and so on.

For example, you are negotiating with Franco and Geraldine. You might ask, "What will it take to get this deal done?" Although Franco claims to be the lead negotiator, he looks at Geraldine. You watch Geraldine raise her eyes. Franco replies, "I'm not sure." You recognize that Franco took his signal from Geraldine, which could be an indication that Geraldine is the real power source at the table.

Be aware that good negotiators know that you are watching for these kinds of signals and may attempt to confuse you as to who the real lead negotiator is. Watching the body language will enable you to determine who is in charge and what the other team's strategy might be. Depending on whatever is being negotiated for, you then have more insight about what the other team is willing to do to get you to negotiate more amicably, or back down from your offers and counteroffers.

Signals between partners

Tiffany and Christine had spent a lot of time marketing their wellness programs to a large corporation. They were in a final decision-making meeting with Barbara. Tiffany watched Christine's body language as Barbara reacted to the proposal. Tiffany thought, "Christine is smiling and nodding and looks like she is ready to accept the terms Barbara is proposing. But Barbara is offering us a price that is far below what we quoted her. What's wrong with Christine? We talked about this before the meeting and agreed that we would hold to our proposed price."

Tiffany and Christine could have avoided this situation by setting up signals ahead of time, just like you would if you were on a baseball diamond or on a football field. Let's see how they could communicate with each other with body language. Before the meeting with Barbara, Tiffany and Christine agreed on signals that will indicate certain things. They decided that Tiffany would have the ultimate decision-making responsibility during the negotiation. She would observe Christine's hand movements. Christine would convey her reaction of "I'm displeased with this particular offer" by moving her hand from the table to her lap. Barbara would not likely pick up such a subtle signal.

In the meeting, Christine conveyed to Tiffany that she was not enamored with the offer. Tiffany did not give away through her body language the fact that the offer was not acceptable. Instead, she continued to position herself as the lead negotiator for her team while not disclosing to Barbara that really she was not the power person. When Christine was happy with the offer, she moved her hand from her lap to the table, palm up.

Who is in charge?

Sometimes it serves your purpose to not initially reveal the identity of the power person. Danny and Angelina are negotiating with Eddie to purchase his restaurant. Danny is acting as the lead negotiator. Angelina is the power person and the senior negotiator. Eddie has named a price that is so ridiculous that Angelina emphatically says to Danny, "I think we are wasting our time, Danny. Let's go." When Angelina stands up, Eddie is puzzled. He thought Danny was the lead person, and now discovers that Angelina holds the power.

Danny turns to Eddie and says, "I would love to conclude the deal but Angelina is unhappy with the terms. Let me see if I can talk to her out in the hall." This tactic of good cop/bad cop, which you read about in Chapter 8, makes Eddie realize, "I made a big mistake. I assumed because Angelina is a woman that she was not the power person. This deal is not going to be easy to complete now."

When you are headed to an impasse

What are some signs that would indicate a negotiation is headed toward a roadblock? Watch body language for early warnings. Let's talk about that from a body language perspective first. Guadalupe is negotiating with Rene to purchase an office condominium for her business. Rene leans away from Guadalupe. As Guadalupe attempts to appease her, Rene leans further away. She sent Guadalupe a signal that meant "No. Your offer is not making me come toward you. Instead it's causing me to lean further away. Make a better offer."

Guadalupe increases the price she is willing to pay. As Rene leans further away, Guadalupe thinks, "Are we going to hit an impasse now if I continue to hold to that price? Or is this a ploy Rene is using to make me believe no matter what I offer, she is going to hold out for full price?"

Rene leans forward and says "Do a little bit better and we may have a deal." All the time that she was leaning away she was sending the subliminal message that we may be headed toward an impasse. Rene deliberately assumed this posture to get Guadalupe to put what she perceived to be her best offer on the table. Rene gained insight into how far Guadalupe was willing to negotiate to buy the condominium.

Guadalupe could have used a different strategy when she perceived she was heading toward an impasse. This is what she might have done: She started to slow the pace of the negotiation to see what Rene did next. Guadalupe knew Rene had another meeting to follow their negotiation. Since time was a factor in the negotiation and Guadalupe sensed that they were headed toward an impasse, she slowed down her responses. She watched Rene's body language to determine if she was effectively applying pressure on Rene. Guadalupe asked herself the following questions:

- Is Rene becoming more engaged?
- Is she leaning forward more?
- Are her hands more open?
- Are her arms further away from her body?

The suggestion of an impasse conveyed through subliminal messages can be used in a negotiation to gain insight into how badly the other negotiator wants the deal and what strategies she will employ to get past the potential impasse. Impasses are strategic tools that you may use in a negotiation to gain an advantage.

Offers: Who Goes First?

There are many variables that go into the decision of who should make the first offer in a negotiation. Both parties go into the negotiation knowing what it is that they are seeking, that there are potential road blocks, and that they need to agree on terms.

Dean Howard is a claims adjuster who handles many files. How effective he is in settling one case is not as important as his overall performance in how well he can control costs. Dean is in a stronger position than Ashley Miller, a plaintiff attorney. Ashely handles far fewer files and wants to get as much money as she can for each client. Since Dean is in the stronger position, he opens the negotiation by saying, "Here's the deal that we can put on the table at this time."

Listen to that verbiage. There's a subliminal message: "This is the best deal we can put on the table *at this time*." The unspoken message is, "Yes, we may be able to put a better deal on the table going forth." This is one of the reasons subliminal messages are so important in a negotiation. Dean has set the stage for negotiations.

Let's contrast that with the weaker negotiator trying to act in a stronger position. Ashley says, "We could never accept the deal that I think you would offer. That's why I am sitting in your office to discuss this." The positioning of that statement said in a stronger more fervent manner also indicates that she's trying to say, "This is our position and we are strong."

Dean responds, "Really!" His eyes are wide as he implies, "Come on, don't even try it. That's not going to fly with me." Ashley has weakened her position with her bluster. By making that statement she has put herself a step behind where she would have been had Dean made the first offer.

There are variables that go into who should make the first offer. The person making the first offer will set the tone of the negotiation. You would make the first offer if you are in a strong position or want to communicate your strength. To the degree you want to see what the other negotiator might do, you offer him the opportunity to make the first offer. Base your decision making on the strategy that you have laid out for the negotiation. That determines whether you allow the other negotiator to make the first offer or you will actually make it. The point is that you need to understand based on your strategy why you would allow the other negotiator to make the first offer.

Counteroffers

Don't be a pushover. What do I mean by that? One thing you don't want to do is to continuously make counteroffers that cause you to cave into the other person's wishes for the outcome of the negotiation versus yours. When you make counteroffers that concede points to your opponent, you're showing your weakness. If that's the case, you don't want to send that signal because that encourages your opponent to just continuously ask for more concessions from you.

Take into consideration when making a counteroffer what might be the outcome. Will the other negotiator say yes, will he say no? If he says no, what will be your response? That also goes back to your planning stages. As I discussed in Chapter 3, "Primers," planning helps you anticipate detours and impasses.

The way you make and offer your counteroffers impacts detours around a roadblock in a negotiation. Do not engage in counteroffers haphazardly not knowing where they may lead. If you're not sure, take a time out. Literally get away from the negotiation table.

Earlier I covered silent signals you would plan with a negotiating partner. A time-out signal allows you to get away from the negotiation table if you encounter a situation where you are not prepared to make a counteroffer or you even want to give the impression that you need to think about the other person's offer. Giving the impression that you need time to think about the other person's offer is also a good strategy to employ when making a counteroffer even if you don't have a counteroffer in hand. By giving the impression that you're being deliberate, you provide more emphasis to your counteroffer. One way to slow the possible negative effects of an offer or counteroffer is to ask for some concession from the opposing negotiator. Once she realizes that you'll request something in order for her to get something, you'll put her on notice that she should not be so quick to make requests.

Post-Deal Maneuvers

You have shaken hands, the symbolic nonverbal body language that says, "Yes, we have a deal." But does it really mean that? In some situations, in some cultures, shaking hands at the conclusion of a deal is nothing more than the end of one phase and the beginning of the next. When you shake hands, does that mean the both negotiators agree the deal is concluded?

Always set the groundwork so that you know what is going to follow: "So you're going to do this (specify), correct?" The other negotiator says, "Yes." Continue to summarize the steps to obtain the other negotiator's agreement. Watch the other negotiator's body language when you summarize the agreement. If you're talking to someone on the phone, listen to the words that he uses.

Leslie has just sold licensing fees to Krishna, who works a company that wants to use Leslie's training materials. As Leslie reiterates the deal, Krishna replies, "Yes, I *think* (pause) we can follow up by sending that $100,000 check within the next two weeks." Leslie becomes concerned by the manner in which Krishna spoke. He sounded like he was not sure he could follow through with what is supposed to be the agreement. Leslie replied, "Wait a minute. I'm sensing some form of hesitation. Please, tell me what it is that I'm sensing." A smart negotiator would say, "How can I tell you what you're sensing?" He does not want to disclose his full position at that time.

Leslie realized she needed to have a strategy to ensure that she got her check or get out of the deal so she could work with a different company. She should expect Krishna to react to her apprehension so that the deal stays together and doesn't run the risk of unraveling.

During the negotiation process, observe body language to determine to what degree your opponent is in agreement with you. At the conclusion of the negotiation, if you have sensed that he was not in agreement about a specific point, bring the point up. Why would you want to raise it? Will you run the risk of unraveling the negotiation? Rather, you enhance the probability of the negotiation staying intact by raising a point of potential contention and addressing it at that time instead of allowing it to fester.

In Summary

Buyer's remorse in a negotiation stems from someone accepting some aspect of the negotiation during the negotiation process that he did not completely agree with. He thinks he could have done a better job negotiating to get a better outcome. This raises the risk that the negotiator will look for a reason to get out of the deal. Reduce the chances of buyer's remorse in the other negotiator by reviewing the terms of the agreement and proactively addressing any unresolved points.

Be aware of all the parties that you're negotiating with, even if they're not at the negotiation table. Address each point that could cause the deal to unravel, why it might unravel, and to what degree the other party is satisfied with the deal that's on the table. By doing so you will enhance the probability of having a successful negotiation and create better negotiation outcomes for yourself.

Chapter 10

* * * * * * * * * * * *

Strategies: *Putting It All Together*

As the other negotiators entered the room, Mike Kim observed their body language. "Jose Mendez looks nervous. He won't make eye contact, and he keeps clicking the top of his pen," he thought. "Gary Porter radiates confidence. He is smiling broadly and looking around the room." Mike took charge of the meeting by outlining the value of the business he wanted to sell. Jose made notes and asked questions from the list he prepared ahead of time. Gary wrote no notes, but he glanced at Jose's notes when asking questions. Mike watched their facial expressions. When he saw puzzlement, he clarified his presentation. When he sensed he was presenting too much information, he backed off and slowed down. At the end of the session, they had a deal.

Controlling Signals

Your ability to control your signals can have a profound impact on a negotiation. Jose sent a signal that he was nervous. Although his nervousness made him alert, it also could be used against him by the opponent who perceived him as stressed. Contrast that with how Gary was open, relaxed, and acted as though he had not a care in the world. The message he sent was, "If we get the deal, great. If we don't get the deal, we'll live." Jose sent a signal that was the exact opposite; he projected the image of needing the deal. A savvy negotiator needs to be concerned about controlling the verbal and nonverbal signals that he sends in a negotiation because they set the tone for the negotiation.

The body language signals you convey through your body language and what you say at the beginning influence what happens during the negotiation. They set the tone for what follows. An astute negotiator observes your body language to draw conclusions about how you feel at the beginning of the negotiation and watches how your signals change based on the discussion and the offers being made.

Misleading Body Language

I just said you should match your body language with your desires. At times, you may deliberately *mislead* your opponent through using body language signals that do not represent what you are thinking or feeling. For example, you might project happiness with an offer he's put on the table even though you may sense it's detrimental to your position. You would watch to see what he might do next then, all of a sudden, change your body language to express displeasure with the offer. Your opponent will be confused and ask himself: "Hey, wait a minute; what exactly is this guy trying to do? What is he really seeking from the negotiation?"

When you use body language, not only do you have to be astutely aware of *why* you're doing it, you also have to be very astutely aware of *how* you are being perceived.

Suppose Gary intentionally came into the negotiation room radiating confidence, smiling broadly, and looking around the room while appearing to be completely relaxed. His deliberate signal was, "I don't have a care in the world. This negotiation can come about successfully or not. I have a backup position. I'm going through the motions here. I'm just granting you the privilege of spending time with me."

By projecting a carefree image, Gary is preventing his opponent from understanding his interest in the deal. He could leave Mike wondering, "Does this guy really want this deal? I wonder if I'm wasting my time. How will he react the way I try to influence him based on my strategy? Will I have to make some big concessions to get him interested?"

Mike should definitely observe how Gary's demeanor is altered as they go throughout the negotiation. How do Gary's body language and statements change based on the offers and counteroffers? And to what degree are they aligned with his strategy?

Measuring Progress with Observations

Make an assessment as to how well the negotiation is progressing based on what you thought would occur at different points in the negotiation. Contrast body language and the strategies that have and have not occurred with offers that your opponent accepted and dismissed.

Mike watched the facial expressions of Jose and Gary, and he realized that he may have been giving too much information. Here is what to observe to get that type of insight:

- Is your opponent shaking or nodding his head?
- Is he patting the table or looking around when you are speaking?
- Is he eagerly sitting on the edge of his seat as an active participant in the discussion, or is his posture expressing the desire to expedite the discussion?
- From a body language perspective, you observe him sitting on the edge of the seat. Look for clusters of signals. Is he also tapping his fingers, clicking a pen, or doing something else that gives you more insight into his impatience?

You observe your opponent looks attentive but his eyes are glazed. You wonder, "To what degree am I even getting through to him? Is he bored? Am I going too fast? Am I being too complex? How should I determine if he is following me?" Make sure that he is following you, but then if he starts asking one question after another, you know he may be seeking more information. Observe his body language and his messages. Note not only the word choices he makes, but also the questions he asks. This will help you determine if you are giving too much or not enough information.

Microexpressions

In Chapter 2, you read about the importance of watching your opponent's face for quick flashes of emotion. In particular, watch his eyes. Do they start to become a little wider as he talks about an offer or counteroffer? Does he frown? All of those are signals that a negotiator can observe if he is astute enough.

Microexpressions give you insight into your opponent's mindset, particularly when you are both discussing an offer.

"Having a poker face" is an expression that means you give away no emotions. It is challenging to try to maintain a poker face. You may recall childhood games of trying to make a friend laugh who was attempting to maintain a poker face. Inevitably, your persistence won out.

Microexpressions are true expressions of someone's state of mind for that one second that it takes for a microexpression to be expressed. That's why microexpressions provide such great insight into another person's thoughts even though she is trying to project a poker face. The mind does not have a chance to filter before the expression is displayed. If she displays a microexpression and then returns to her previous facial expression, you know she is intentionally trying not to give away any insight about her thought process.

One thing you can say in such a situation is, "I understand that you're not in agreement with anything that I'm going to say." Watch what happens. She might maintain her poker face and stop talking. You could both be silent. But eventually if you stay there long enough the other person is going to say, "Okay, what else do you have to say?" to resume the discussion.

Let's say literally hours will go by and she does not say anything. Provided you are patient enough to wait, you would get even greater insight as to how determined she is to maintain her poker face. This will give you insight as to how receptive she might be to accepting or rejecting an offer you make.

Negotiating Against Yourself

Has this ever happened to you? You go to an auction for the first time and get handed a little paddle with a number on it, which you use to signal your bid. The auctioneer asks, "I've got $5, do I hear $10?" You really want that item but lose track in the middle of the auction and find yourself bidding against yourself. With a withering glance, the auctioneer tells you, "You had the last bid."

This type of trap may occur in a negotiation. You are negotiating with your opponent. You see her smile; you keep talking and her smile becomes broader. You are sweetening the offer. All of sudden, you realize you have given up too much ground. You have fallen into the trap of negotiating against yourself. Stop talking. At least get her input as to what she thinks about the offer that you've put on the table.

Negotiating against yourself may occur when you give out too much information. Here is what might happen: You make an offer: "$1,000 is the best that I can do." The other negotiator doesn't say a word. You think, "I really want this deal. His silence worries me. How can I get the deal?" You say, "Maybe I can go up to $1,500." Again, the other negotiator doesn't say anything. You're negotiating against yourself; his silence should have been a sign not to say anything. Pause when you have not gotten any response.

Suppose the opponent gives you a big, broad smile at a point when you offer $1,000. You may have just offered too much. Be cautious as to how you make your offers and watch your opponent's body language. That same smile could be interpreted as, "Wait a minute, this offer is way better than I expected." This is why you have to be cautious when, why, and how much information you give.

How do you know you are correctly interpreting body language? Instead of rushing into a situation in which you are bidding against yourself, seek feedback. Ask some probing questions. "What do you think about that?" "How does that sound to you?" "That's a good offer, isn't it?" (while nodding your head in approval because it's a good offer in your favor).

A Team Approach

In the chapter's opening scenario, Jose and Gary worked as a team during their discussion with Mike. They played good cop/bad cop. Jose was extremely uptight. Gary acted blasé. Jose was the one taking notes. Gary looked at Jose's notes to pose his questions. They were watching Mike's reactions.

Who was the dominant person in the situation? Who was the real power figure and to what degree were they representing their position in order to be secure in going forward in the negotiation? Gary projected the role he was playing being carefree, as if to say, "I'm not even taking notes. This doesn't mean that much to me. What did Jose write? Oh yeah, that was something I wanted to ask just because I needed to gather more input."

Both Jose and Gary consistently played their roles. That's why I said as you enter into a negotiation, observe how your opponent's demeanor is altered as the result of the offers and counteroffers that are made. Thus, you know how to better position your offers.

This is something that occurred that made me really question how in control a leader can be of his team when he and the team are negotiating. A new governor had just taken office. My team and I had a meeting with the governor's secretary of commerce. I had already prepped the team by telling them about the objective I wanted to attain: We wanted to position ourselves as essential to the governor.

The secretary of commerce was new to his position. Everybody on my team understood his or her role and the outcome we were seeking. Everybody on my team indicated they understood I would be the lead person. I would do the majority of the talking and ask the majority of the questions when we got into the meeting with the secretary. In our meeting the secretary started to speak when I was talking. I would not relinquish the floor to him.

Now, understand the dynamics. I was a regular citizen. We were sitting in an impressive conference room. We were meeting in a power room with a secretary who was appointed to a magnificent role by the governor. I would not relinquish the floor to him. He tried to speak. I kept speaking if he tried to interrupt me. If he was speaking, I interrupted him. The reason I was doing that was to use a negotiation ploy to show I was the dominant person in the negotiation.

My team had rehearsed what would be said; everybody agreed to his or her role. Nevertheless, a member of my team said, "Greg, don't interrupt him. Let him talk." I threw a glare at him that made the room go so cold the chief of staff for the secretary literally said, "Wow, it really got chilly in here." My team member and I had an emphatic talk after the meeting.

Even in a controlled situation where you think you have everything in hand, in a team environment when you're negotiating expect the unexpected. To the degree that people play their roles, the negotiation will progress much better with the strategies you put in place in your planning process. If somebody throws a monkey wrench into the situation, you have to react as a leader. From that point on I never invited that person to another session that I was involved in. Burned once, twice shy.

Those are some of the dynamics you have to be very much aware of in a team environment. If you are the junior person sitting in on a negotiation, you may wonder, "Wait a minute, what is going on? Why is the team leader doing that?" Don't speak up. Sit there and be quiet per the role you're supposed to play. Everybody has to understand their role in a team environment.

Body Language in a Successful Negotiation

As I just stressed, a successful negotiation is created in the planning stage. Determine what it is that you want in the form of the outcome that you're seeking from the negotiation. Take into consideration what the other negotiator wants from it and what you and he will both agree to. Put all of those components into your planning process.

Ask yourself, "What will occur if I say X and he says Y? We start to agree on Z and something happens there. Do we go back to A?" Anticipate how to react to detours in your planning process. Observe how he is reacting to your offers and counteroffers. Does he grimace? Does he pull away by leaning away from the table when you make an offer? Look at all those body language signals when you're in a negotiation to determine to what degree your plan is successfully received.

Create a roadmap for how you will engage in the negotiation. You also set mile markers as to where you should be at any point per the offers and counteroffers that have been accepted or rejected in the negotiation. Note if your opponent's body language is consistent with your plans.

Also observe how you are feeling. Do you feel the onset of a sudden headache? Is your stomach tight? Are your hands clenched? Tune into your own body language as well as your opponent's. Do you need a time-out? Do you need to slow down the pace of the discussion? By noting your own reactions, you can make decisions about switching tactics. Make sure that you have procedures in place so if you can't get what you need from that negotiator you have another source to go to. That allows you to not feel so stressed in the negotiation that you can convey your emotions in your body language.

Bluffing has its advantages. Suppose you are negotiating with a man. He says, "Look, that's my best offer. Take it or leave it."

Without saying a word, you get up and start moving away from the table. He cries, "Wait a minute, where are you going?"

You: "You said take it or leave it. I'm going to leave it."

Him: "Look, tell me what you need me to do to make it a little better offer."

Now you have him on the defensive. Make sure you understand what a successful negotiation will entail to put your plans in place for the body language signals you will use. Smile at the appropriate time. Smile even at the inappropriate time to make the opponent wonder about your agreement with the offer he is making. All of these are aspects you have to consider in a negotiation. The body language you project will play a crucial role not only in a planning but also in carrying out a negotiation.

Always remember the value of planning. Recall how I planned the negotiation when I talked to my team before meeting with the governor's secretary of commerce. Plan the negotiation with role playing to anticipate the questions you might be asked. Use this strategy to test the effectiveness of your plan and determine how you might alter it. By planning and role playing you also get the opportunity to have a real-life experience without having to pay the cost of the same experience at the negotiation table.

Emotional Intelligence in Negotiations

Emotional intelligence drives planning and carrying out negotiations. As I discussed in Chapter 6, know your hot buttons, the triggers that will make you react in certain ways. What are your opponent's triggers?

Emotional intelligence is interwoven with body language. Your hot buttons and triggers are activated before you are aware of it. Microexpressions are visible before your brain has a chance to stop them from displaying emotions you are experiencing.

Know what will set you off from an emotional intelligence perspective. For example, when I need to negotiate with a company over a customer service issue I get annoyed when I have to wait on hold for a long time. I am already irritated by the time the person picks up the phone. I get even more irritated by finding out I have been waiting on hold for the wrong department. And if I get switched to three or four departments, I am ready to blow my top. This insight leads me to exercise control over myself so that I don't take out my frustration on the person who is trying to negotiate with me.

Consider the same risk of anger when you are in a face-to-face negotiation. Control your microexpressions to the degree you can. Be aware of the microexpressions you might convey: fear, anger, disgust, surprise, contempt, sadness, or happiness. Recognize the potential for giving away something about your mind-set; your thought process are revealed to your opponent through microexpressions.

If you understand from an emotional intelligence perspective what you are triggered to say and do based on a stimulus, you know you need to be on guard against this. Be on the alert for comments that are designed to manipulate you. For example, your opponent says, "If you don't get this deal, you're going to lose your business." Hide your fear. When you have anticipated this tactic, you can rehearse your reaction and not get rattled. That's an aspect of emotional intelligence. To the degree that emotional intelligence may influence body language you have a degree of control.

Framing the Negotiation Environment

Framing involves considering optics. Know what you are trying to achieve. Recall I gave an example in Chapter 6 about how Allen Carter ushered his opponent, Terrence Titler, into the private dining room at his exclusive club room at the race-track. Allen wanted to project an air of success and convey this message: "This is an upscale environment." He knew Terrence wanted to obtain the status of being someone who would fit into that environment.

You may recall Allen actually tested Terrence by allowing a hint of condescension to creep into his voice. "Of course you know, Terrence, taking care of a horse involves feed, training, and vet bills. Are you *sure* you are prepared for the expense?" Allen's probing sent the message: "Wait a minute, this might cost a little more than you thought." Terrence took the bait and reassured Allen it would be no problem.

Suppose Terrence hunched his shoulders as he said that. Terrence was trying to bring his head into his shoulder to make himself a smaller target. From a body language perspective, this expression said, "There may be problem." When you're framing the environment for the negotiation, take into consideration how you can position the other negotiator to be most advantageous to your negotiation efforts. How do you do that?

- Does that mean having it in an upscale environment?
- Does it mean that you are wearing certain clothes or colors?
- Does it mean your jewelry projects an air of success?

All of those are questions that you pose to yourself when determining how you're going to frame the environment to influence the opponent. Just as you recognize the optics that work in your favor, so also might your opponent. Be alert to the fact you may be talking in someone else's environment. Your opponent had the same opportunity to frame it to her advantage. You can dismiss that if you choose to. Suppose the negotiation is in an opulent place. You might walk in with an attitude that conveys: "Is this the best you got?" Right away you have taken away some of the other person's power and informed her that you are not going to be influenced by her optics. Thus, framing does play an important role in the negotiation from both perspectives—how to use it as an advantage and how to position it as a disadvantage to the other negotiator.

Adjusting the Framing

Clearly you could incorrectly frame a situation. You start off with one intention in mind and quickly realize your set of expectations or environment is not going to work to your advantage. You can always suggest you switch venues. The other person could inquire, "Why do you want to switch venues?" You reply, making it sound as if you are concerned for the opponent: "I just thought you will feel more comfortable in a different environment."

You will recall in Chapter 3 you read about Stephen Woodruff, who deliberately made the temperature in the room colder than Bonnie Mallick preferred. She commented on how cold it had gotten. When she acquiesced to an offer or a counteroffer, Stephen got the temperature increased. Let's say Bonnie was aware or suspected that somebody was manipulating the thermostat. Once she saw the correlation between her behavior and the temperature, she said to herself, "I'm not going to react like one of Pavlov's dogs. I am going to ignore the temperature and pretend I am completely comfortable." Seeing his scheme fall apart, Stephen thought, "This is not having the effect that I wanted it to have on the negotiation. Bonnie has figured out I'm manipulating the temperature. I better try something else."

Noting Stephen was trying to manipulate her, Bonnie said, "How about if we just go to another venue?" Stephen asked,

"Why do you want to go a different place?" Bonnie needed a plausible reason for her request. "These chairs are uncomfortable. I have a back problem. Let's move to that room down the hall." Your responses are driven either by your planning, experiences encountering manipulation of the environment, or on-the-spot adjustments in strategy.

This is something else Bonnie could do: "Stephen, I notice that whenever I disagree with your offers you make the room colder. Why is that?" Stephen needs to have a plausible explanation: If Stephen is being truthful, he would say: "Bonnie, I did that to entice you to be predisposed to my offers. I apologize. Please forgive me." (He's throwing himself on her mercy since she caught him at his ploy.) If Stephen is being untruthful or strident, he'd say: "Bonnie, I don't know what you're talking about. If you observing correlations between your offer and counteroffers and the temperature in the room, maybe you want to think about being fairer."

Power Letters and Phrases

Display your confidence with power letters and phrases. Power letters are hard sounding: D, G, K, P, M, and T. Soft letters are S, H, F, and L. Think about the power letters in "Go get this deal done." Power letters influence how you word some of your sentences. Use hard consonants and letters to emphasize points and soft ones to downplay others.

Power phrases indicate to what degree you are confident about the offer or counteroffer that you're making or your sense of where the negotiation is headed.

Power phrases convey authority. Make your point and stop. Power phrases say what you mean. They are direct. Not, "That's OK, don't worry about it" but "This is a problem. We need to find a solution" or "I need your help to resolve this."

- Avoid filler phrases: "Well," "sort of," "I would tend to," "I guess," and "I'm not sure about this." Replace indecisive phrases with decisive phrases.
- Avoid phrases that deflect due credit ("I was lucky" and "it was nothing") with phrases that accept credit ("I worked hard, thank you.")
- Speak with assurance. If you cannot be certain about some aspect of a deal, express what you *can* be certain about.
- Accept credit and compliments.
- Avoid negative phrases: "I am really sorry, I hope you will consider what I have to offer. I know it is not very much." Frame your messages in positive terms. "I am confident you will be happy with this offer."

Consider the impact of power letters and phrases in a negotiation. Couple them with body language that reiterates your power. For example, you point at yourself as you say, "We can deliver on our promise." The body language of pointing at yourself while aligning your words with that action conveys authority.

Contrast this with Caron Michaels, who says, "We can definitely help you achieve the goals you're seeking." At the same time she says that, instead of pointing, Caron leans away from the table. Her body language is indicating with the gesture of leaning away, "I don't really want to be associated with this statement that I just made because I'm not that sure of it myself."

You observe Caron's body language is not synchronized with the words she is using. You can also gain insight that Caron is attempting to use power words, but something is not right. The degree of confidence Caron displays in those words does not match the body language she is exhibiting; thus, you should follow the body language.

In addition, you can also test Caron's conviction about the power words she is using. Caron said, "We can definitely give you what you want from this deal." You can then paraphrase her and say something like, "Really?" See what she says. Does she reiterate her comment or back down? With one word, "really," you can determine if she is trying to use power words that she cannot substantiate.

Take it a step further and say, "You said you *think* you can guarantee you will be able to give me what I want from this deal." Notice I added the words "you think." Observe how Caron responds through her body language and words. Does she pause and say, "Uh-h-h yes"? That little pause between "Uh-h-h yes" gave you insight through her body language that she was not 100 percent sure.

Silent Stakeholders

Let's return to the topic of silent stakeholders, which I discussed in Chapter 3. Recall the scenario I presented at the beginning of this chapter. What would happen if one of the men did not have the authority to conclude a deal without the other. If we change the situation, now Jose is present but Gary is not. Mike is talking to Jose, who looks nervous. Mike probes to find out why Jose is so nervous. "Jose, I see you are nervous. What is bothering you? Do you have the ability to conclude a deal today?"

Jose says, "Well uh-h yes, yes." While Jose's voice said "yes," his body language gestures said "no." At that point Mike might say, "I hear what you're saying, but you didn't sound very convincing. Who else is actually involved in this negotiation that you would have to consult in order to conclude a deal?"

The question "who else" is an assumptive question, meaning there's somebody else who is involved in the negotiation and not present. The assumption could be completely wrong, but

Mike allows Jose to think Mike knows a little bit more than Jose does. Mike scrutinizes Jose's body language as he stammers, "Uh-h nobody else is involved in it."

Mike notes Jose's pause. Jose has just sent a signal that he has to think about the answer he's going to give. Mike asks, "Really?" Jose admits, "I have to talk with my colleague Gary." Now Mike has identified the other stakeholder. He replies, "Can we get Gary on the phone right now?" Mike wants to make sure all the stakeholders are involved so the deal can be concluded. Gary has now been pointed out as the silent stakeholder. This is why you should always ask the question who else is involved in this negotiation who has a stake in it.

Let's reverse the scenario. Instead of Jose being at the negotiation table, Gary is in the room without Jose. In looking at Gary, Mike sees his demeanor: "I can care less if we get this deal concluded. I am just here just to go along to get along." Mike confronts Gary: "Who else is involved in this negotiation who might need to have input?" Let's say Gary casually replies, "Nobody." If by chance Mike is not 100 percent sure he believes Gary that no one else is involved in the negotiation, it would still behoove him to probe early about this in the negotiation.

Mike clarifies, "Let me understand this, Gary; if we are able to come to a conclusion today on an agreement for the negotiation, you will be able to sign the agreement today. We will have a deal. Is that correct?" At that point Gary has to either be very truthful or he has to decide that he's going to lie. Even in the time that it takes Gary to respond to that, Mike can gain some insight.

Gary looks up and to the left. As you read in Chapter 1, looking up and to the left indicates Gary is more likely searching his past. (Always assess how people use their body language before the negotiation to accurately detect signals in the negotiation.) His body language says, "Wait a minute. Let me see. Is there anybody else who needs to be considered in this?" He already knows that there is or isn't somebody, so why does he go through that thought process? While watching Gary's face, Mike asks, "Really?" Gary responds, "There is my colleague Jose." "What input does Jose have in this whole deal?" Mike asks. The answer to this question gives Mike an understanding of the effect of Jose's absence on the negotiation. Mike will continue to probe until he finds out to what degree Jose is actually an integral part in the negotiation.

Optics and Negotiation

Optics become a strategic part of a negotiation; they play a huge role in a negotiation. They set the tone and put you in the proper mind-set for a negotiation. These questions may arise:

- "Does my opponent have the right demeanor given what's being negotiated?"
- "Is something off in this situation?"
- "Is something occurring in the environment I should be aware of?"

One time I was in the process of going to a lawyer's office to hire him. The reason I was going to his office as opposed to talking to him over the phone first is because I wanted to see his natural environment. I was curious about what the office looked like, who was really working there, what they were doing, and how much activity was going on. Before I left home, I took off my expensive watch and college ring. I did not want to give him any clues about my financial well-being; I wasn't giving away anything. Let's say the attorney was only going to charge me $150 an hour for his services. If I left my watch on, he might have recalculated his fee and thought, "This guy can probably afford $200 to $250 an hour." He may have adjusted his rate on the spot. I did not give him that opportunity.

When it comes to setting the right environment, anticipate what a person expects to see. If you go to a lawyer's office who charges $600 an hour, you would not expect the office to be dingy, quiet, dimly lit, or have pictures on the wall of dogs playing cards. The optics of that would be the wrong environment for the $600 an hour lawyer. Your negotiation is affected by the environment in which you negotiate.

Status symbols play a big role in optics—people form impressions about you based on your jewelry and cars. Defense attorneys tell physicians accused of medical malpractice to not drive to the courthouse in their expensive cars for fear that jurors will notice and assume the physician is able to afford a large judgment. There are so many facets that optics create at a negotiation that you always have to be very much aware of their strategic role.

You decide your next car is going to be a Chevrolet. You drive up to the dealer in a Lexus, Mercedes, or Jaguar. What have you done? You've sent a signal, "Hey, I've got money." Car salespeople are attuned to observing cars potential buyers drive. If you're driving up to a Chevy dealer's lot in a Mercedes, the car salesperson figures he can show you the highest-priced models and negotiate with you a little more stringently.

When There are No Good Choices

What do you do when you're in a negotiation and feel trapped? The answer is in the planning stage. If you have ever gone to an auction, you have seen people swept up in the excitement of bidding. Envision two people who are locked in a battle. Each wants the item, but at one point, one of them has to drop out. Never get so caught up in the negotiation that you lose any gains you might have realized. Planning a negotiation is like going into an auction knowing how far you are willing to go to get an item. When you plan the outcome of the negotiation, have a ceiling as far as what's the best you can get from the negotiation. You need to have a midpoint: "If I reach this point, I'm happy." What is your floor? That's to say, if the deal does not meet this criteria you will walk away from the negotiation and not tie your emotions to the negotiation.

Here's where emotional intelligence also comes into play. Always be willing to walk away from a negotiation. In so doing you will be insulating yourself from staying engaged in the negotiation if by chance you are below the lowest offer you know you can accept. Calculate what you're going to walk away from. Be willing to tell your opponent, "This is not going to be satisfactory for us today. How about we reconvene later?" You can gracefully get away from the negotiation, but the one thing you don't want to do is berate the other negotiator: "Oh, you're such a jerk. I can't believe you would make such an insulting offer. I would never negotiate with you again. I can't believe your parents actually had you. What a disservice they did to the world when they gave birth to you!" Don't say anything along those lines because that is not a graceful exit at all. Always leave the negotiation door at least cracked just a little bit so you can go back in and reopen the negotiation. Don't burn any bridges.

You can state with a smile on your face, "I really appreciate the fact that you and I have engaged in the negotiation with an honest and open perspective." You're complementing the other negotiator. Let's say the other negotiator really wasn't that open and honest. You're still setting the boundaries by which you would be suggesting, "Let's negotiate a little more fairly and honestly."

In Summary

I've gone through a lot of the aspects that make for a successful negotiation and negotiator. Be aware of what body language signals and nonverbal signals mean. Recognize the need to be emotionally tuned from an emotional intelligence perspective about the use of triggers.

Once you know which microexpressions to look for, you will gain greater insight into your opponent's emotions. Use all of these aspects of a successful negotiation. You will become a much more astute, skilled, and successful negotiator and win more negotiations. Then everything will be right with the world.

INDEX

THE AUTHOR

Greg Williams, "The Master Negotiator and Body Language Expert," has taught negotiation and reading body language skills to people worldwide. The practical content in this book is driven by the author's deep knowledge of negotiation principles and body language. Greg is a TV news contributor and an internationally known and sought-after speaker. As a business owner since 1993, Greg has gained an extensive background in management and business operations. He is an author and presenter who has mastered the fine art of negotiation and reading body language, and is a worldwide recognized public speaker and trainer on those subjects.

Through seminars, coaching, and training, Greg educated tens of thousands of individuals on how to become better negotiators. He enabled them to increase their emotional intelligence, while using the ability to read body language to enhance the process. Greg's reach extends to government and corporate settings. He has also negotiated many multimillion-dollar deals on behalf of some of his clients.

As an author, coach, trainer, and keynote speaker on the subject of negotiations and reading body language, Greg has become a recognized expert in the field. He has appeared on numerous TV and radio programs, discussing negotiation tactics and strategies that anyone can use to achieve higher outcomes in every negotiation. He's done this while coupling the added benefit of how to read body language while negotiating.

For those who are serious about discovering how to read body language and achieving more in life by becoming better negotiators, Greg also created audio and video programs and other tools (http://www.themasternegotiator.com/tags/greg-williams-the-master-negotiator-body-language-expert/).